The development of the 8-Radwagen, or eight-wheeled armoured car, which would eventually become the Sdkfz 234 series of vehicles, was an attempt to capitalise on the mobility, speed and range of the Sdkfz 231 which had been in service since the beginning of the war. These early designs had shown the value of a fast-moving vehicle with all-wheel steering but they were lightly armed and had been conceived with the temperate climate of northern Europe in mind.

By 1941, with the commitment to North Africa and the invasion of the Soviet Union, the reconnaissance elements of the German army found themselves operating in barren, often hostile, environments and these units were almost always at the forefront of any advance and were regularly forced to fight their way forward, a task for which the light armament of the pre-war designs was ill suited. The introduction in July 1942 of the 7.5cm-armed Sdkfz 233, the first of which were allocated to units destined for Tunisia, went some way towards remedying this but the development of the Sdkfz 234, which offered simplified design features, a lower silhouette and greater mechanical reliability, was well underway by that time (1).

In the first part of this series (2), we considered the Sdkfz 234/3 and Sdkfz 234/4 and in this book we will analyse the technical aspects of the Sdkfz 234/1 and 234/2, the models which entered service first and also accounted for the bulk of production. The contrast in their intended missions can be seen by comparing the official tables of establishment (3) presented in the first part and those rendered on pages 60, 61, 62 and 63 of this book.

The fact that armoured cars were usually found at the Schwerpunkt, or the point of main effort, meant that relatively few were photographed and the reader will notice that many of the images in this book depict captured or abandoned vehicles. The comparatively small numbers of Sdkfz 234 vehicles produced, and their late introduction into service, also contributed to this.

The illustrations presented in this book and the remarks made regarding camouflage colours were all based on contemporary photographs and official documents but are essentially my interpretations and where aspects are the subject of debate I have endeavoured to make this obvious.

To create a clear picture of the development and use of the Sdkfz 234/1 and 234/2 it was essential that some information from the first book, particularly that concerning allocations, is repeated in this volume and I trust readers will forgive this. I should also mention that I have deliberately avoided the use of the term Puma although there is some evidence, as mentioned in the note on page 14, that it was in fact employed during the war.

Notes

1. The Sdkfz 233 was not a new design but a conversion based on an existing model. It was as much an attempt to utilise the surplus 7.5cm L/24 guns as it was to create an effective weapon system.

2. *LandCraft 11: Pakwagen Sdkfz 234/3 and 234/4 Heavy Armoured Cars, German Army, Waffen-SS and Luftwaffe Units, Western and Eastern Fronts, 1944–1945.*

3. Referred to as Kriegsstärkenachweisungen, abbreviated to KstN.

Said to have been photographed on the Oder Front in early 1945, the Sdkfz 234/1 armoured car at right is accompanied by several Sdkfz 251/1 halftracks and another armoured car visible in the distance. The insignia on the rear access door of one of the halftracks, although obscured, is similar to that used by 25.Panzergrenadier-Division and that unit was allocated two Sdkfz 234/1 vehicles in February 1945 and took part in the fighting around Küstrin, modern-day Kostrzyn nad Odra on the Oder River, eventually withdrawing to Berlin.

SDKFZ 234 PRODUCTION, 1943-1945

Accurate production figures for the Sdkfz 234 series armoured cars are not available but we can gain some insight into the monthly totals by examining the numbers of vehicles accepted by the Heereswaffenamt and the allocations to training establishments and combat units. The latter is examined in detail on pages 58 and 59. Where I have been forced to use approximations I have tried to make this clear.

	Sdkfz 234/1		Sdkfz 234/2		Sdkfz 234/3		Sdkfz 234/4	
	Accepted	*Allocated*	*Accepted*	*Allocated*	*Accepted*	*Allocated*	*Accepted*	*Allocated*
August 1943			1 (1)					
September 1943			2 (2)					
October 1943								
November 1943								
December 1943			4 (3)	1				
January 1944			5	5				
February 1944			12	12				
March 1944			22	18				
April 1944			30	23				
May 1944			19	17				
June 1944	(4)		7	18	(4)			
July 1944	12 (5)	45	2 (6)	2		13		
August 1944	(7)	7			(7)	6		
September 1944	(8)	41	2	1	(8)			
October 1944	35	29		2	1	16		
November 1944	27	25		5	13	12		
December 1944	11	15		3	17	23	25	25
January 1945	37	26		3 (9)			3	18
February 1945	22	11					26	22
March 1945	18 (10)	18					17 (11)	6 (12)
April 1945		17						

1. Trial vehicle. 2. Trial vehicle. 3. The first series production models. 4. In this month a total of fifty-three Sdkfz 234/1 and Sdkfz 234/2 vehicles were accepted but unfortunately there is no detailed breakdown and they are merely recorded as Panzerspähwagen. The allocation of forty-five Sdkfz 234/1 versions would suggest that type made up the bulk of the delivery. 5. This number also represents Sdkfz 234/1 and Sdkfz 234/3 models. 6. At least one of these vehicles was returned from repair. 7. In this month a total of thirty-one Sdkfz 234/1 and Sdkfz 234/2 vehicles were accepted but again there is no detailed breakdown. 8. In this month a total of forty-one Sdkfz 234/1 and Sdkfz 234/2 vehicles were accepted but there is no detailed breakdown. 9. This number is provisional and the last allocation of these vehicles may have been the three assigned to 7.Panzer-Division in the previous month. 10, 11 and 12. These figures are all approximations.

An Sdkfz 234/2 armoured car of 1.Kompanie, Panzer-Aufklärungs-Abteilung 2 photographed in France during the summer of 1944. Other vehicles of this battalion are shown on page 18 of the Camouflage & Markings section and the numbering system is explained on page 62.

The first examples of the Sdkfz 234/2, commonly referred to today as the Puma, were allocated to training units in September 1943 and it was intended that these vehicles would equip the reconnaissance battalions of Panzer divisions that were to be reorganised according to new Kriegsstärkenachweisungen (KstN) establishments by early 1944. The Sdkfz 234/1 with its 2cm gun in an enclosed turret was designed to replace the lightly-armoured scout cars that had been in service since the beginning of the war and, in terms of numbers produced, this model was the most important version of the Sdkfz 234 series. The following text gives brief histories of the units that were equipped with these large armoured cars but it should be mentioned that the numbers given here, and in the charts on pages 58 and 59 indicating vehicles assigned to certain units, have for the most part been taken from the Zuhführungliste, or shipping lists, and while these are consistently accurate, even those recorded in the last weeks of the war, they do represent vehicles assigned and not necessarily those that arrived. Where this is known I have tried to make it clear. The references made here to KstN and other organisational terms are explained in detail in the final section of this book which begins on page 60. Units which operated the other vehicles of this series, the Sdkfz 234/3 and 234/4, were examined in *LandCraft 11: Pakwagen, Sdkfz 234/3 and 234/4 Armoured Cars German Army, Waffen-SS and Luftwaffe Units Western and Eastern Fronts 1944-1945* and are listed here with the notation 'See LC 11', for the sake of completeness. There is of course some overlap between the two groups and I trust readers will forgive any repetition. The abbreviation PzAA, for Panzer-Aufklärungs-Abteilung, or armoured reconnaissance battalion, is used throughout this section.

1.Panzer-Division. See LC 11.

2.Panzer-Division. The division's PzAA 2 was formed on 16 March 1943 by renaming Kradschützen-Batallion 2. The division fought on the Eastern Front and by the end of the year had been transferred to France to be rebuilt. At this time PzAA 2 was reorganised according to the KstN issued in November 1943 and this is shown in the chart on page 60. Although the battalion received orders in May 1944 to re-establish its companies in line with the frei Gliederung principles that were introduced in the previous month it appears that this did not take place before August. At the commencement of the battles in Normandy the battalion was under the command of Major Bernhard von Schkopp and 1.Kompanie, organised according to KStN 1162a of 1 November 1943, contained a full complement of twenty-five Sdkfz 234/2 armoured cars. This formation was one of just two battalions that received their complete allocation of these vehicles (1). The numbering system employed by 1.Kompanie was quite unusual and is explained in the diagram on page 62.

Most accounts suggest that the battalion was completely destroyed during the fighting for the Falaise Pocket in August 1944 but in the first week of the following month the commander reported that nine Sdkfz 234/2 vehicles were still on hand but were now with the battalion's Stabskompanie. Their placement proves that the reorganisation to the April KstN had taken place or had at least begun. A number of accounts mention that a single Sdkfz 234/1 and three Sdkfz 234/3 armoured cars were also with the Stabskompanie but the division never received any of these vehicles before November 1944 and the armoured cars in question were actually Sdkfz 233 and Sdkfz 232 models.

In November 1944 the battalion was rebuilt and in the same month two Sdkfz 234/1 and two Sdkfz 234/2 were shipped from the Heereszeugamt (2). It is possible that the latter were vehices taken over from Panzer-Lehr-Division. During the Ardennes Offensive the battalion formed the nucleus of a large Kampfgruppe led by Hauptmann von Böhm (3) that was reinforced with tank and armoured infantry units as the battle progressed.

At that time the Stabskompanie contained the eleven Sdkfz 234/2 and two Sdkfz 234/1 armoured cars that the battalion possessed. In addition there were a number of Sdkfz 233 and Sdkfz 232 vehicles and three armoured halftracks. Interestingly the Sdkfz 234/2 armoured cars retained the numbering system that was used by 1.Kompanie in Normandy. Kampfgruppe von Böhm formed the division's spearhead and was able to advance further than any other German unit, reaching the area between Foy-Notre-Dame and Dinant on the morning of 24 December 1944. But there they were cut off by British armoured units and Hauptmann von Böhm and 147 men of his Kampfgruppe were taken prisoner and PzAA 2 effectively ceased to exist.

In 1945 an attempt was made to rebuild the division by merging the remnants with Panzer-Ausbildungs-Verband Thüringen, an ad-hoc unit made up principally from training units stationed at Bergen, with PzAA 2 but no further allocation of armoured cars is recorded (4). Vehicles of PzAA 2 are depicted on pages 18 and 21 of the Camouflage & Markings section of this book.

4.Panzer-Division. Formed by renaming Kradschützen Battalion 34 on 30 April 30 1943, the division's PzAA 4 retained the November 1943 organisation of a headquarters and five companies throughout the war. During January 1945 the battalion was withdrawn from the front and at that time was allocated one Sdkfz 234/1 and six Sdkfz 234/4 armoured cars. These probably arrived in mid-February and were all assigned to the battalion's 1.Kompanie (5). In the same month the battalion also received sixteen Sdkfz 250 armoured halftracks. In March 1945 the battalion was consolidated with PzAA München (see below). A vehicle of PzAA 4 is depicted in the Camouflage & Markings section of this book on page 24.

Notes

1. The other formation was the reconnaissance battalion of the Panzer-Lehr-Division.
2. The Heereszeugamt was the army's supply directorate.The last heavy armoured cars did not arrive until April 1944.
3. This officer is something of a mystery. In most accounts he is mentioned as the commander of PzAA 2, replacing Major von Schkopp in August 1944, but does not appear in any of the surviving division lists nor in the comprehensive *Deutsche Truppen im Zweiten Weltkrieg Band 2* which covers, among other units, 2.Panzer-Division. An award document dated October 1944 suggests that Major von Schkopp was still with the battalion at that time but he was attached to Panzer-Brigade 106 by early January 1945 at the latest.
4. Interestingly, Hauptmann Walter Helmut, the commander of Panzer-Ausbildungs-Verband Thüringen, was nominated for the award of the Ritterkreuz on 9 May 1945, one day after the official German surrender.
5. There is some debate over these figures with at least one authoratitive source stating that the shipment was made up of seven Sdkfz 234/1 vehicles.

At left and below:Sdkfz 234/2 armoured cars of 1.Kompanie, Panzer-Aufklärungs-Abteilung 2 photographed in Normandy during the summer of 1944. This battalion, and Panzer-Aufklärungs-Lehr-Abteilung 130, were the only units to receive a full allocation of twenty-five of these vehicles. Variations can be seen in the application of the Balkenkreuz national insignia with some rendered as white outlines only while most have a dark centre section. On some vehicles, notably 1.Truppe, the Balkenkreuz was placed behind the turret number. The colour used for the centre of the numbers is a matter of longstanding debate with some sources suggesting that they are red while others state that they are black. My personal feeling tends toward the latter.

Although not visible here, the Truppe numbers, in this case 5 and 11, were repeated on the side of the mudguard on the first locker door. The numbers were rendered in white for the first vehicle of the Truppe and in black for the second. The unusual numbering system and its meaning is explained in detail on page 62. All vehicles were painted in a base coat of RAL 7028 Dunkelgelb, the factory standard of the time, and camouflaged with RAL 8017 Rotbraun and RAL 6003 Olivgrün in patterns made up of random strokes and swirls and examples are shown on pages 18 and 21 of the Camouflage & Markings section.

6.Panzer-Division. In June 1944 the division's PzAA 6, less 4.Kompanie, was being rebuilt at Bergen in Germany and at that time was allocated three Sdkfz 234/3 armoured cars. In August three Sdkfz 234/1 vehicles were shipped by the Heereszeugamt (1) and in the following month another ten armoured cars of the same type were despatched. The Sdkfz 234 series vehicles were all assigned to the Stabskompanie and the other companies were equipped with Sdkfz 250 halftracks. The battalion returned to the front and took part in the defence of Vilnius in Lithuania and the fighting along the Bug and Narew Rivers in East Prussia.

By early December 1944 the division had been moved to north-west Hungary and was engaged in the defensive battles around Budapest and the subsequent attempts to relieve the German garrison. In early 1945 the battalion was involved in the defence of Vienna. The survivors retreated towards the west and surrendered to units of the US Army at Jihlava, north-west of Brno in Czechoslovakia, but were handed back to the Soviets. An Sdkfz 234/1 armoured car of PzAA 6 is shown on page 23 of the Camouflage & Markings section of this book.

7.Panzer-Division. The division's PzAA 7 was created on 1 April 1943 by renaming Kradschützen-Bataillon 7. The battalion was allocated six Sdkfz 234/2 armoured cars in February 1944 and was the first combat unit to receive the type. These heavy vehicles were all concentrated in 1.Kompanie until July 1944 when the battalion was reorganised and the Sdkfz 234/2 armoured cars were assigned to the battalion's Stabskompanie (2).

By the autumn of 1944 the division was engaged in the defensive battles in Lithuania and Latvia, most notably around the port city of Memel, present-day Klaipeda. The survivors of the division were evacuated to Pillau in Germany by sea at the end of 1944 and moved to the training centre at Arys in East Prussia where the battalion was rebuilt. It was probably at this time that three further Sdkfz 234/2 vehicles were received. In mid-January 1945 the division returned to the front and took part in the defensive battles between Soldau and Elbing and eventually withdrew towards Danzig, modern-day Gdansk in Poland. Forced with a number of other formations into the Oxhöfer Kämpe, a large cliff formation on the Bay of Gdansk, the division was again evacuated by sea, leaving all its heavy equipment behind.

The last remnants of PzAA 7, possibly enough to form a company-sized unit, fought as infantry against British troops around Mecklenburg and many of these may have been men of 3.Kompane, PzAA 12 which was transferred to the battalion in late April 1945. Vehicles of PzAA 7 are depicted on pages 19 and 22 of the Camouflage & Markings section of this book.

8.Panzer-Division. The division's PzAA 8 was reorganised according to the April 1944 frei Gliederung KstN establishments and in August of the same year was allocated three Sdkfz 234/3 armoured

Notes

1. The allocation of these vehicles is not mentioned in some accounts and disputed in others but the presence of these Sdkfz 234/2 armoured cars during the summer of 1944 is verified by photographic evidence.

cars. In the following month thirteen Sdkfz 234/1 vehicles were shipped to the battalion, bringing it to its full authorised strength. In January 1945 the battalion reported that fifteen heavy armoured cars were still on hand and as no Sdkfz 233 vehicles (1) were issued to this unit these must be survivors of the August and September shipments.

In February 1945 the battalion contained eighteen heavy armoured cars, all concentrated in the Stabskompanie, and four companies equipped with Sdkfz 250 halftracks. In March 1945 a total of four heavy Panzerspähwagen (2) were shipped to the battalion and these may have been Sdkfz 234/4 armoured cars.

9.Panzer-Division. The complete division, with PzAA 9, was withdrawn from the Eastern Front in April 1944 and reorganised using the frei Gliderung KstN establishments. In June, PzAA 9 was allocated thirteen Sdkfz 234/1 armoured cars and in July three Sdkfz 234/3 vehicles were shipped and these were all assigned to the battalion Stabskompanie. This unit was also authorised a reconnaissance company formed with KstN 1162b, the fully-tracked version, equipped with the Pzkpfw II ausf L Luchs. The division suffered heavily in the Normandy battles but by September 1944 had been rebuilt to almost full strength, reporting that five Sdkfz 234/1 and three Sdkfz 234/3 were on hand. In the same month the division took part in the fighting south of Aachen and in October 1944 was subordinated to II.SS-Panzerkorps for the assault on the Nijmegen bridgehead. In November 1944 a total of ten Sdkfz 234/1 and two Sdkfz 234/3 armoured cars were dispatched by the Heereszeugamt but the former were delivered to 9.SS-Panzer-Division and it is unclear if this was as a result of an administrative error or simple opportunism. In any event this was the last allocation of heavy armoured cars made to the battalion. This left PzAA 9 with three Sdkfz 234/1 and a single Sdkfz 234/3 vehicle and by the end of November the battalion had undergone an unofficial reorganisation with the heavy armoured cars removed from the Stabskompanie and placed in 1.Kompanie with the remaining six Pzkpfw II tanks. The division was rebuilt for the Ardennes Offensive and although its losses in this operation were light, the vehicle strength of PzAA 9 was far below its authorised allocation. The heavy armoured cars were still with 1.Kompanie and one Sdkfz 234/3 had been added and as there is no record of any new allocation, this may have been a vehicle returned from repair.

In early 1945 the division was defending the West Wall positions between Erkelenz and Erft and gradually fell back into Cologne were it was involved in house-to-house fighting. By the first week of March 1945 PzAA 9 had been almost completely destroyed.

Notes

1. The Sdkfz 233 was an earlier eight-wheeled armoured car armed with the 7.5cm gun. Production eneded in October 1943 but many were still in service when the war ended.

2. Literally, heavy armoured scout cars. Unfortunately the Zuhführungliste often refer to allocations using this generic term only without mention of a specific type or model.

Captured German equipment photographed at the Allied collection point at Celles, south-east of Dinant in Belgium, after the Ardennes Offensive. The Sdkfz 234/2 armoured car in the background, one of several that were operated by Kampfgruppe von Böhm, was shipped to the United States after the war and is in fact the vehicle shown on page 9. Other images clearly show the small brackets welded to the turret sides and a field-modified handle fitted to the hull forward access door, all identifying features of Panzer-Aufklärungs-Lehr-Abteilung 130 armoured cars.

Unfortunately the Red Army photographer who took this image recorded very little information about the vehicles location. German researcher Martin Block has suggested, based on a comparison of registration plate numbers, that this is one of the Sdkfz 234/2 armoured cars allocated to Panzer-Aufklärungs-Abteilung 7. This vehicle is also shown in the Camouflage & Markings section on page 22.

11.Panzer-Division. Formed in April 1943, the division's PzAA 11 was rebuilt in May 1944 by the addition of Reserve-Panzer-Aufklärungs-Abteilung 7. In June 1944 a total of thirteen Sdkfz 234/1 armoured cars was shipped to the battalion and the July allocation of three Sdkfz 234/3 vehicles brought the battalion to full strength. In August 1944 the division took part in the fighting in southern France, slowly withdrawing towards the north-east.

At the commencement of the battles in Lorraine in September this was probably the strongest German armoured unit on the Western Front but by the beginning of December the division had suffered such heavy losses that its participation in the Ardennes Offensive was limited to Heeresgruppe reserve. Elements of the division, particularly PzAA 11, were engaged in the attacks against the Remagen Bridgehead.

13.Panzer-Division. The division's PzAA 13 was completely destroyed in the summer 1944 battles on the Eastern Front and rebuilt in November according to the April 1944 KstN frei Gleiderung establishments.

Prior to this, in September, the division had been renamed Panzer-Division Feldherrnhalle. In December 1944 the battalion was allocated two Sdkfz 234/3 armoured cars and was at that time heavyily engaged in the defence of Budapest. A report compiled in the same month lists eight armoured cars of all types with twenty-two Sdkfz 250 halftracks on hand. The division was trapped in Budapest and the few men that were able to escape were used to build Panzer-Division Feldherrnhalle 2 from February 1945. The Zuführungliste records that seven Panzerspähwagen were shipped to 13.Panzer-Division in March 1945, possibly four Sdkfz 234/1 and three Sdkfz 234/4 armoured cars, but these probably went to Panzerkorps-Feldherrnhalle (1).

17.Panzer-Division. The division's PzAA 17 was formed in May 1943 and had been equipped with Sdkfz 250 and Sdkfz 251 armoured halftracks. As a result of the consolidation with PzAA Hirschberg in March 1945 this battalion became one of the division's strongest assets with a Stabskompanie, built on the 1944 KstN, controlling the heavy armoured cars, in addition to two halftrack companies, two light reconnaissance companies and a heavy support company.

The surviving division's Gliederungen, or organisational charts, for March and April 1945 specifically mention that two 'Pz.Sp.Wg Luchs II' were on hand and although this would seem to refer to the Sdkfz 123 light tank, commonly referred to as the Luchs or Lynx, there is no mention in any allocation list of these vehicles being shipped to the division. It is unlikely that the tanks came from any of the other units serving in the East at that time but one possible candidate is PzAA Hirschberg as it was formed from units of the Ersatzheer (see Panzer-Brigade 103, below). Although tenuous, this may go some way towards explaining the conversion based on an Sdkfz 234 hull fitted with a Luchs turret shown on page 26 of the Camouflage & Markings section of this book.

Notes

1. It is interesting that this formation is referred to as 13.Panzer-Division at this late date as there is anecdotal evidence that the Feldherrnhalle honour title, and its association with the National Socialist Sturm Abteilung, was not popular.

20.Panzer-Division. The division's PzAA 20 had been reduced to two companies by the end of 1943 and was withdrawn from the front and sent to Wildflecken in Germany to be rebuilt. In June 1944 the battalion was allocated sixteen Sdkfz 234/2 armoured cars and at the end of July PzAA 20 returned to the East. It did not rejoin its parent formation but acted as an independent Heerestruppe unit, for the most part subordinated to 5.Panzer-Division.

In September 1944 a total of three Sdkfz 234/3 armoured cars were shipped to the battalion and it was noted that the sixteen Sdkfz 234/2 were still on hand. In the following month the battalion returned to 20.Panzer-Division which was being refurbish at Truppenübungsplatz Arys in East Prussia.

In January 1945 the division was moved to Hungary and took part in the fighting for the Gran Bridgehead but within weeks the German positions here had been abandoned and 20.Panzer-Division was transferred to the area around Sosnowitz, modern-day Sosnowiec in Poland, after the Russians had been able to create a salient on the western bank of the Vistula. After heavy fighting the division withdrew across the Oder River on 31 January 1945 and held the defensive line here north of Ratibor, today Raciborz.

In mid-February the division took part in the attempt to relieve the fortress of Breslau and managed to hold open an escape coridor for two days but was eventually pushed back and withdrew to Landskrone, south of Görlitz. In April 1945 elements of the division were fighting around Pulsnitz and Königsbrück in order to hold back the Soviet units advancing towards Dresden but slowly began retreating towards the south, into Czechoslovakia, and then west.

A report dated 1 April 1945 shows that PzAA 20 had one Sdkfz 234/3 (1) and ten sdkfz 234/2 armoured cars on hand, all with the Stabskompanie. At that time the battalion had no 3.Kompanie and 4.Kompanie was without any motor transport.

During the first week of May 1945, while bulk of the division retreated towards the West and the approaching US Army, the remnants of PzAA 20 were ordered to relieve the German garrison in Prague. But after radio communication was lost, the last units of 20.Panzer-Division headed towards the West and surrendered to units of the US Army near Pilsen, present-day Plzen in the Czech Republic.

A series of photographs taken of the event show the Stabskompanie and at least three Sdkfz 234/2 armoured cars and an Sdkfz 233 7.5cm-armed vehicle are visible. Also depicted is one of the battalion's Sdkfz 234/3 models fitted with a 2cm Schwebelafette mounting, presumably taken from an Sdkfz 251/17 halftrack (2). Vehicles of PzAA 20 are shown in the Camouflage & Markings section of this book on pages 22 and 25.

23.Panzer-Division. See LC 11.

24.Panzer-Division. Formed in April 1943, the division's PzAA 24 was organised using the 1943 KstN and did not officially adopt the frei Gleiderung establishment until 5 January 1945, although there is some evidence that

Notes

1. Some sources suggest this vehicle was in fact an Sdkfz 233 and one of these heavy armoured cars had in fact been taken over from 273.Reserve-Panzer-Division in May 1944.
2. The 2cm Schwebelafette conversion is examined in some detail in *LandCraft 11: Pakwagen, Sdkfz 234/3 and 234/4 Armoured Cars German Army, Waffen-SS and Luftwaffe Units Western and Eastern Fronts 1944-1945.*

At right: Photographed near Pilsen, in the modern-day Czech Republic, probably outside the village of Ejopovice on the road to Prague, these vehicles are from Stabskompanie, Panzer-Aufklärungs-Abteilung 20. In the series of photographs and the film made of the event, at least three different Sdkfz 234/2 armoured cars and an 2dkfz 234/3 vehicle are visible. All appear to be in good condition with few parts damaged or missing. Note also the conversion based on an Sdkfz 234/3 fitted with a 2cm Schwebelafette gun mount parked behind the civilian car.

At left: Another Sdkfz 234/2 armoured car of Stabskompanie, Panzer-Aufklärungs-Abteilung 20 photographed when the remnants of the battalion surrendered to units of the US Army during the first week of May 1945. Note the camouflage netting fixed to the turret, the number 024 and the position of the Balkenkreuz. Vehicles of this battalion are shown on page 25 of the Camouflage & Markings section of this book. The figure in the foreground of our photograph is Hauptmann Petersmann, the last commanding officer of the battalion.

parts of the battalion were reorganised before that date. It is worth mentioning that the battalion's Stabskompanie was the only such unit in the German army organised according to the 1945 KstN. In December 1944 the Heereszeugamt shipped three Sdkfz 234/3 armoured cars to PzAA 24 and in the following month another seven Sdkfz 234/3 vehicles and a further eight Sdkfz 234/1 models were sent.

On 12 January 1945 the division was moved rapidly from the area of Heeresgruppe Süd to East Prussia, leaving most of its heavy equipment behind, and it is likely that the fifteen vehicles received in that month made up the battalion's heavy component. The division took part in the defensive battles in Ermland on the Baltic coast and the retreat to the bridgehead near Heiligenbeil. At the end of March 1945 the surviving elements of 24.Panzer-Division were evacuated by sea to the Frisches Haff near Pillau, modern-day Baltiysk, again losing most of their heavy equipment.

25.Panzer-Division. The division's reconnaissance element, PzAA 25, was largely destroyed in February 1944 and in July the rebuilding of a new battalion began. Organised using a modified version of the April 1944 KstN establishments, the battalion was equipped with light armoured cars and Sdkfz 250 halftracks. By March 1945 the division had been reorganised as Kampfgruppe 25.Panzer-Division and in the same month PzAA 25 was allocated four Sdkfz 234/1 and three Sdkfz 234/4 armoured cars, not quite enough to equip a single platoon.

116.Panzer-Division. The divison's PzAA 116 was formed in late April 1944 and organised according to the 1944 frei Gleiderung KstN with a Stabskompanie and four companies. In June a total of thirteen Sdkfz 234/1 and three Sdkfz 234/3 armoured cars were shipped to the battalion and these were assigned to the Stabskompanie.

The division fought in the battles in Normandy and was badly depleted, a strength report of 20 August 1944 making no mention of the Stabskompanie or the heavy armoured cars. The battalion also suffered heavy personnel losses, including Hauptmann Kurt Zehner, the commander, killed in the last week of July 1944. In the following September PzAA 116 reported that just three armoured cars and thirty armoured halftracks were on hand but in the same month the division absorbed the remnants of Panzer-Brigade 108 and many of the vehicles went to PzAA 116.

A report compiled on 8 November 1944 states that the Stabskompanie contained nine Sdkfz 234/1 and two Sdkfz 234/3 armoured cars and a shipment later that month increased the total by four Sdkfz 234/1 and a single Sdkfz 234/3 vehicle, raising the company to its full authorised strength. The other companies were equipped with various models of the Sdkfz 250 and Sdkfz 251 halftrack. In early 1945 the division took part in the defence of the Roer River dams and narrowly escaped encirclement at Wesel, north of Duisburg, after withdrawing across the Rhine and destroying the only bridge in the area. In the fighting here Feldwebel Fritz Muster, commanding one of the battalion's heavy armoured car Truppe, deliberately drew an enemy attack onto his own position with the intention of luring the American tanks to within range of a battery of 8.8cm anti-aircraft guns. While the Flak battery engaged the Allied armour, later claiming to have destroyed sixteen tanks, Feldwebel Muster located the remnants of a Sturmgeschütz company and led the assault guns in a counterattack. For his bravey and initiative Muster was awarded the Ritterkreuz, one of three such presentations made to members of PzAA 116 during the last weeks of the war.

In April 1945 the Heereszeugamt shipped six Sdkfz 243/4 to PzAA 116 although these may have eventually gone to PzAA Döring of Panzer-Division Clausewitz (1). The majority of the division was trapped in the Ruhr Pocket and surrendered on 18 April 1945 near Lippstadt although some elements managed to break out (2).

Panzer-Lehr-Division. The orders to create this formation were issued in December 1943 and it was intended that the division would provide a testing ground for the anticipated frei Gleiderung establishments. New KstN were authorised on 1 March 1944 and most of these were simply numbered as KstN fG von 1 November 1943, followed by the unit's title or description (3).

In June 1944 the division's Panzer-Aufklärungs-Lehr-Abteilung 130 (PzALA 130) was organised according to the 1943 KstN with a Stabskompanie, four reconnaissance companies and a heavy support company. This battalion had been created from the Aufklärungs-Lehr-Abteilung (ALA), an instructional unit based at Krampnitz outside Berlin.

Oberst Helmut Ritgens, who served with the division, stated in his post-war history that the battalion's 1.Kompanie contained four troops, each equipped with four Sdkfz 234/2 armoured cars, with a further two vehicles in the headquarters troop. This is exactly the number of this model that were allocated to ALA up to March 1944 and has been confirmed, although the official authorisation was for twenty-five. But the thirteen Sdkfz 234/1 and three Sdkfz 234/3 vehicles that Oberst Ritgens mentions as authorised for the Stabskompanie were not on hand in June 1944 and deliveries of the former would take some time while the latter never materialised. The division fought in the Normandy battles and PzALA 130 was the

Notes

1. It is also possible that this shipment did in fact contain two heavy armoured cars and four light vehicles as mentioned in an order of 7 April 1945 which called for the creation of Kampfgruppe 116.Panzer-Division.
2. In his history of the division, published in English as *From Normandy to the Ruhr: With the 116th Panzer Division in World War II,* Heinz Günther Guderian states that the last soldiers of the division surrendered in the Harz mountain region, south-east of Hannover. Guderian served as the division's chief of staff and operations officer and was of course the son of Generaloberst Heinz Wilhelm Guderian, the Generalinspekteur der Panzertruppen.
3. The 3 August 1944 order which introduced the Panzer-Division 44 organisation and called for the general application of the frei Gleiderung establishment mentioned that special arrangements applied to Panzer-Lehr and 21.Panzer-Division

first element to make contact with the enemy on Sunday, 11 June 1944 near Ellon, south of Bayeaux, where a serious firefight developed which soon involved the Panthers of Panzer-Regiment 6. The battalion suffered its first casualties here and seven halftracks and one of the Sdkfz 234/2 armoured cars were completely destroyed.

On 25 July 1944 Panzer-Lehr-Division was caught in the massive aerial bombardment that preceded Operation Cobra, the American breakout from the Normandy beaches, and PzALA 130 was the worst-affected element of the division. It was originally intended that the battalion should participate in Operation Lüttich, the only large-scale German counterattack of the campaign, but it was instead assigned to protect the southern flank of the assault, directly under the command of XXXXVII.Panzerkorps.

By 20 August 1944, at the conclusion of the fighting for the Falaise Pocket, the battalion had been reduced to 150 men and eight armoured cars (1). The division was temporarily renamed Kampfgruppe Panzer-Lehr and was made up of a number of smaller Kampfgruppen including a unit commanded by Oberst Paul Freiherr von Hauser which contained the surviving elements of PzALA 130.

By early October most of the battalion's heavy equipment, including a number of Sdkfz 234/2 armoured cars, were handed over to PzAA 2 and what is almost certainly one of these vehicles is shown on page 21 of the Camouflage & Markings section. The battalion was rebuilt in October 1944 and at the end of the month PzALA 130 was allocated a number of Sdkfz 234/1 armoured cars (2). In the following month another two Sdkfz 234/1 models were shipped and these arrived on 8 November. Oberst Ritgens mentions that four Sdkfz 234/2 vehicles had survived the Normandy battles and were still with the battlion but there is some argument over the accuracy of this statement.

In December 1944 the division took part in the Ardennes Offensive and in the early weeks of 1945 was involved in the battles along the Lower Rhine and the attempts to destroy the American bridgehead at Remagen. The last remnants of the division surrendered in April 1945 after being trapped in the Ruhr pocket. Vehicles of PzALA 130 are depicted on pages 19 and 20 of the Camouflage & Markings section of this book.

Panzer-Division Feldherrnhalle. See 13.Panzer-Division.

Führer-Begleit-Division. This formation was raised from the Führer-Begleit-Brigade on 26 January 1945 and contained Panzer-Späh-Kompanie 102 which was renamed Führer-Panzer-Späh-Kompanie 2 in March. In late January 1945 the company had twenty-one armoured cars of all types on hand and in the following month four Sdkfz 234/1 and six Sdkfz 234/4 vehicles were shipped by the Heersezuegamt. But by 2 March the company had been disbanded and its equipment had disappeared from the division's order of battle.

Panzer-Division Jüterbog. See LC 11.

Panzer-Division Schlesien. See LC 11.

Panzer-Divison Holstein. See LC 11.

Notes

1. Unfortunately the report from which these figures are taken does not specify the model or type of armoured car.

2. The Zuführungsliste shows a shipment of three schwere Panzerspähwagen sent on 24 October with a further seven allocated on 29 October but actually despatched on 5 November 1944. The total of course is ten but a number of authoratative sources insist that true figure was eight vehicles.

Photographed in March 1946, this Sdkfz 234/2 armoured car is the vehicle of Kampfgruppe von Böhm shown in the background of the image reproduced on page 5. Years of exposure to the elements wore away the coat of camouflage paint to reveal the Balkenkreuz and turret number visible here. The handle on the hull access door and the small brackets on the turret side were identifying features of the armoured cars of Panzer-Aufklärungs-Lehr-Abteilung 130 and this may be one of vehicles relinquished by Kamfgruppe von Hauser in November 1944 as mentioned in the text.

Another Sdkfz 234/2 armoured car of Kampfgruppe von Böhm abandoned after the Ardennes Offensive in late December 1944. Note the large wooden stowage box on the rear of the left side mudguard. This was an identifying feature of Panzer-Aufklärungs-Abteilung 2 vehicles and was incorporated prior to the Normandy campaign.

Panzer-Division Müncheberg. Formed on 5 March 1945, this formation was built around Stab, Panzer-Brigade 103, led by Generalmajor Werner Mummert, and Panzer-Abteilung Kummersdorf. On 8 March 1945 the division's reconnaissance element was created from a company that had been detached from PzAA Sternberg which had been subordinated to 10.Panzergrenadier-Division.

Generalmajor Mummert, who had been awarded the Ritterkreuz as the commander of an Aufklärungs battalion early in the war, complained that this unit was totally inadequate as it was equipped throughout with VW light cars and the detachment was later reinforced with four Sdkfz 234/1 and four Sdkfz 234/4 armoured cars and a number of lighter vehicles.

On 11 March 1945 the company was officially renamed Panzerspäh-Kompanie Müncheberg. The battalion took part in the defence of Berlin where all its equipment, and most of its personnel, were lost.

10.Panzergrenadier-Division. See LC 11.

20.Panzergrenadier-Division. In October 1944 the division's PzAA 120 was allocated four Sdkfz 234/1 and two Sdkfz 234/3 armoured cars. In December the division was withdrawn to Kielce in southern Poland but in January found itself defending the city.

On 17 January 1945 the Germans abandoned Kielce and the units of 20.Panzergrenadier-Division retreated first to Lodz then on to the area north-west of Sprottau, modern-day Szprotawa in western Poland, which was part of the Oder-Neisse defensive line. In March 1945 the battalion was detached from the division and sent to Milowitz in Czechoslovakia to be rebuilt.

By this time PzAA 120 had been reduced to the armoured car platoons of the Stabskompanie and the battalion was briefly referred to as Panzerspäh-Kompanie 120. In April 1945 orders were issued that the battalion was to be reformed according to the 1945 KstN lists but it is unclear if this ever took place.

25.Panzergrenadier-Divison. This formation suffered heavy losses in the summer and autumn battles of 1944 on the Eastern Front and was rebuilt around a Kampfgruppe of the original division and the remnants of Panzer-Brigade 107. The division's PzAA 125 was organised according to the April 1944 KstN but with just two light reconnaissance companies equipped with VW light cars

The division fought in the West until January 1945 when it was transported to the Oder Front by rail, taking part in the defence of Küstrin. In February 1945 a total of two Sdkfz 234/1 and a single Sdkfz 234/3 armoured cars were shipped to the battalion which also gained an additional light company and a motorised heavy company.

In April 1945 the divison was allocated six Panzerspähwagen and these were probably two heavy armoured cars and four light vehicles but the exact types are unknown. A vehicle of PzAA 125 is depicted in the Camouflage & Markings section of this book on page 23.

Panzergrenadier-Division Brandenburg. The division's PzAA Brandenburg was formed in September 1944 and was supposed to be organised according to the April 1944 KstN although some sources suggest that it contained just three companies. In October the battalion received just three Sdkfz 234/3 armoured cars, although a total of ten heavy Panzerspähwagen were assigned, and four Sdkfz 234/1 in the following December.

A shipment in January 1945 contained two Sdkfz 234/2 and seven Sdkfz 234/4 vehicles although the allocation of the former is a matter of considerable debate. In mid-January, at the commencement of the Red Army's Vistula-Oder offensive, the battalion's Stabskompanie reported that all these vehicles were operational.

Panzergrenadier-Division Kurmark. Formed from Kampfgruppe Langkeit on 30 January 1945 on Hitler's personal order, this formation never exceeded the strength of a reinforced brigade. Although much of the division's personnel strength was made up of stragglers, convalescents and men returning from leave, the core of veteran officers and NCOs were able to generate an incredibly high degree of proficiency and this formation led the breakout from the Halbe Pocket when German troops were encircled there in late April 1945.

The reconnaissance element was created from PzAA 151, which was renamed PzAA Kurmark, and this unit was in fact a mixed company with the original order for the divison's creation calling for '1 Aufkl.Schwadron (ohne Fahrzeuge)', that is without vehicles. In some accounts it is referred to as Panzerspäh-Kompanie Kurmark but this may have been a misinterpretation of the official March 1945 Kriegsgliederung which called for a Stabskompanie, a Panzerspäh-Kompanie and a Panzer-Aufklärungs-Kompanie. On Friday, 2 February 1945, five Sdkfz 234/1 and three Sdkfz 234/4 armoured cars were shipped to the battalion and these had arrived by the following Monday. The division was thrown into the fighting around Frankfurt an der Oder but was withdrawn by the end of March.

The division returned to the frontline on 16 April 1945 but was forced to retreat within days and was eventually encircled in the Halbe Pocket were PzAA Kurmark was almost completely destroyed (1).

Panzer-Brigade 103. Originally formed on 21 July 1944, the brigade was engaged in the battles in the Baltic States, particularly around Tukkum on the Gulf of Riga, and was moved to East Prussia in September taking part in the fighting around Gumbinnen and Schlossberg, halting a major Soviet advance in front of the village of Ebenrode, modern-day Nesterov in Russia.

The heavy fighting took its toll and by the first week of November 1944 the brigade staff, with the personnel of the Panzer battalion and the maintenance platoon, were moved to Bielefeld in western Germany and the remaining vehicles were handed over to 5.Panzer-Division. In late November the brigade staff served on the Western Front as the headquarters of Kampfgruppe Führer-Begleit-Brigade and from 20 January 1945 the staff was used to coordinate a Panzer Kampfgruppe which was made up of the first battalions of Panzer-Regiment 29 and Panzer-Regiment 39 and the second battalion of Panzer-Regiment 9 (2).

Notes

1. Some elements of the division managed to reach the Elbe River and surrendered to units of the US Army.

2. In some accounts this formation is referred to, somewhat confusingly, as Kampfgruppe Panzer-Brigade 103 and although a number of the brigade's personnel were certainly present, it should not be considered a reformed or resurrected version of the original brigade.

Said to have been photographed near the Elbe River in May 1945, this Sdkfz 234/1 armoured car was probably assembled during December 1944 when the simplified mudguards were introduced into production but just prior to the adoption of a factory-applied camouflage scheme. If the location is correct, this vehicle may be one of the heavy armoured cars assigned to 25.Panzergrenadier-Division or Panzergrenadier-Division Kurmark in February 1945 but any attempt at identification at this stage of the conflict can only be speculation. This vehicle is also shown on page 26 of the Camouflage & Markings section.

An Sdkfz 234/1 armoured car parked near the Church of Saint Mary Magdelene in the town of Chvalsiny, in what is today the Czech Republic. Chvalsiny is situtated south of Winterberg, modern-day Vimperk, on the edge of the Bayerischer Wald national park, and the remnants of Panzerkorps FHH and 25.Panzer-Division, both of which operated a number of these vehicles, retreated through this area in May 1945. This vehicle is also shown on page 25 of the Camouflage & Markings section.

PzAA Hirschberg, which had been formed from 1.Kompanie, PzAA 190 and elements of Panzer-Aufklärungs-Ersatz und Ausbildungs-Abteilung 55, was also subordinated to Stab, Panzer-Brigade 103 in January 1945. Earlier, in December 1944, eight Sdkfz 234/1 and one Sdkfz 234/3 armoured cars were shipped to PzAA 190 and in January 1945 one Sdkfz 234/1 and two Sdkfz 234/3 vehicles were allocated.

In March 1945 the brigade was disbanded and the surviving elements of PzAA Hirschberg were absorbed by the reconnaissance battalion of 17.Panzer-Division. Interestingly, organisational charts for the division dated 1 March and 1 April 1945 both state that two 'Pz.Sp.Wg Luchs' were on hand with the reconnaissance battalion, apparently referring to the Sdkfz 123 light tank, although none appear on the official allocation lists. It is possible, although far from certain, that these vehicles came from PzAA Hirschberg and that the turret of at least one was fitted to an Sdkfz 234 hull. The brigade also controlled PzAA Sternberg which was equipped for the most part with VW light cars.

Panzer-Brigade 150. This formation was specifically formed to take part in Unternehmen Greif, the deception operation planned for the Ardennes Offensive. The original plan called for elements of the brigade, disguised as American soldiers, to capture the bridges across the Meuse at Amay, Andenne and Huy on the Liège to Namur road. Under the codename Rabenhügel, the brigade was organised into three Kampfgruppen referred to as X, Y and Z and although each was supposed to have been outfitted with captured US Army vehicles and equipment, only a few armoured cars, halftracks and lorries were available when the offensive began. The few men who spoke fluent English were grouped into a company-sized unit commanded by Hauptsturmführer Horst Stielau which also contained most of the functioning American equipment.

In November 1944 the brigade received three Sdkfz 234/2 and three Sdkfz 234/3 armoured cars and these were all assigned to the Aufklärungs-Zug of the brigade headquarters. The brigade was withdrawn from the front on 28 December 1944 but at least one official document mentions a Kampfgruppe Panzer-Brigade 150 in action during the early months of 1945 as under the command of Hauptmann Walter Scherf, who had led Kampfgruppe Y, and this unit almost certainly contained the surviving armoured cars.

Führer-Grenadier-Brigade. Officially formed on 10 July 1944 as Kampfgruppe Führer-Grenadier-Brigade, this formation was made up from elements of Ersatz-Brigade Grossdeutschland and men of the Führer-Grenadier-Bataillon, a unit of Hitler's bodyguard. The brigade underwent a number of organisational changes during its brief history, some rather confusing (1). During the fighting in the Ardennes in December 1944 the brigade headquarters contained an Aufklärungs-Kompanie equipped with six Sdkfz 234/1 armoured cars, which had been shipped in the previous September, and a number of Sdkfz 250 halftracks.

Notes

1. The organisation is explained in some detail in *TankCraft 24: Panther Tanks: Germany Army Panzer Brigades Western and Eastern Fronts, 1944–1945.*

From 22 December 1944 the brigade was involved in the fighting around Bastogne and the battles for the city of Luxembourg where the commander, Oberst Hans-Joachim Kahler, was seriously wounded. On 16 January 1945, with the offensive halted, the brigade was withdrawn from the front line and reformed as the Führer-Grenadier-Division although its basic organisation remained unchanged.

The reconnaissance company was detached from the headquarters and renamed Panzer-Späh-Kompanie 101, changed in March to Führer-Panzer-Späh-Kompanie 1, and the division served on the Eastern Front until the end of the war.

Radfahr-Jäger-Brigade 10. See LC 11.

Panzer-Aufklärungs-Abteilung 190. In December 1944 eight 234/1 and one 234/3 armoured cars were shipped to the battalion's 1.Kompanie and in January 1945 one 234/1 and two 234/3 vehicles were allocated. In early 1945 the company was used to build PzAA Hirschberg which was for a short time subordinated to Stab, Panzer-Brigade 103 and eventually absorbed by PzAA 17.

Panzer-Aufklärungs-Abteilung Sternberg. In mid-1944 it was proposed that 10.Panzergrenadier-Division be reformed as a complete Panzer division and renamed to take the place of 10.Panzer-Division which had been destroyed in North Africa the previous year. But in the event the division could not be spared from the front and was decimated in the fierce battles of July and August 1944. It was withdrawn to Czechoslovakia and then Poland to be rebuilt but only reached the size of a large Kampfgruppe, which included PzAA 110, and did not return to the East until December.

In February the division's reconnaissance battalion was reinforced by the addition of a unit formed from elements of the Heeres-Unteroffizierschule (Panzer-Aufklärer) located at Sternberg in northern Germany which was referred to as PzAA Sternberg. In March 1945 a company of PzAA Sternberg, equipped with VW light cars, was used to form Panzerspäh-Kompanie Müncheberg. This detachment was later reinforced with four Sd.Kfz. 234/1 and four Sd.Kfz.234/4 armoured cars. See also Panzer-Division Müncheberg.

Panzer-Aufklärungs-Abteilung München. Formed on 29 January 1945 as part of the proposed Panzer-Jagd-Brigade 104, this unit was supposed to be furnished with a single Sdkfz 234/2 armoured car from the assets of Panzer-Aufklärungs-Ersatz und Ausbildungs-Abteilung 7, a replacement and training unit, and a number of halftracks from the Heeres-Nachricten-Schule at Halle. Two Sdkfz 234/1 and one Sdkfz 234/3 vehicles were eventually shipped to the battalion from the Heereszeugamt on 1 February 1945 together with seven light armoured cars. Within two weeks the battalion, still understrength, was sent to the front and operated under Heeresgruppe Weichsel and never joined Panzer-Jagd-Brigade 104. On 11 March 1945 PzAA München was disbanded and incorporated into PzAA 4 of 4.Panzer-Division.

Begleitkompanie z.b.V. Also referred to as Begleitkompanie 1, this unit was attached to Kampfgruppe Möws which fought in the battles around Berlin. In March 1945 three Sdkfz 234/1 and three Sdkfz 234/3 armoured cars were shipped to the company and these probably arrived on the first day of April.

Panzer-Aufklärungs-Abteilung Döring. This battalion was created using elements of Panzer-Aufklärungs-Ersatz-Abteilung 3 and a reconnaissance company originally intended for 4.Kavallerie-Brigade (1).

The battalion had been in training at Altengrabow when it was ordered on 13 April 1945 to join Panzer-Division Clausewitz, the last German armoured division raised during the war, which was in the process of formation in the area south-east of Hamburg. As early as the following day the division's reconnaissance element was being referred to as Panzer-Aufklärungs-Abteilung Elbe and a report of 17 April stated that the battalion consisted of a headquarters staff with a headquarters company, a motorized escort company, a Panzerspäh-Kompanie and a Panzer-Aufklärungs-Kompanie. The same report gave the battalion's vehicle strength as two SdKfz 234/1 and SdKfz 234/4 vehicles with a further eight light armoured cars and twenty-nine Sdkfz 250 halftracks.

Although the division was suppposed to be held in reserve it was almost immediately thrown into the fighting around Uelzen, south of Hamburg, and the mobile elements suffered heavily. By 28 April 1945 the division had officially been reduced to a Kampfgruppe and the Aufklärungs-Abteilung was no longer listed on the strength returns.

Panzerkorps-Feldherrnhalle (FHH). This formation was one of the proposed Panzerkorps (neuer Art) that were partly raised from October 1944. Panzerkorps FHH was built around IV.Panzerkorps headquarters, with elements of Panzergrenadier-Division FHH and 13.Panzer-Divison but all these units had been destroyed by mid-February 1945 in the fighting for Budapest. By chance the reconnaissance battalion of Panzergrenadier-Division FHH was refitting at Milowitz in the present-day Czech Republic at the time and escaped the fate of its parent formation.

Reformed by an order of 25 February 1945, the corps headquarters was initially authorised a single Aufklärungs company but a directive dated 20 March changed

Notes

1. This company was organised using KstN 1162c.

At left and below: An Sdkfz 234/2 armoured car of the special Vorausabteilung, or advanced group, formed from elements of SS-Panzer-Aufklärungs-Abteilung 1 in June 1944. The style of camouflage, which partly covers the Balkenkreauz national insignia, is clearly visible here as is the turret number. Note the periscopes of the commander's and loaders hatches, turret lifting hooks, hull stowage locker and the smoke grenade dischargers which are fully loaded.

Commanded by Hauptsturmführer Karl Böttcher who had only recently returned to the battalion, the Vorausabteilung was detached from its parent formation and sent to the front where it was seconded to 12.SS-Panzer-Division. The photographs and film made during this period have led to the incorrect assumption that SS-Panzer-Aufklärungs-Abteilung 12 was allocated a number of these armoured cars

this to a full battalion and the unit was to be formed around 2.Kompanie, PzAA-FHH which was still at Milowitz. As a consequence, the two divisions subordinated to Panzerkorps FHH, referred to as FHH 1 and FHH2, lost their reconnaissance battalions and were to be authorised single companies equipped with Volkswagen light cars, presumably organised under KstN of 1 November 1944. While at Milowitz the battalion had been allocated three Sdkfz 234/1 armoured cars in December 1944 and a further seven followed in March 1945 together with five Sdkfz 234/4 vehicles. Four of the former and three of the latter had been diverted from 13.Panzer-Division.

Renamed Korps-Panzer-Aufklärungs-Abteilung FHH, the battalion left Milowitz on 29 March 1945 although it still lacked most of its authorised armoured halftracks. On arrival at the front the Stabskompanie, 3.Kompanie and 4.Kompanie were split between the two divisions while the other two companies were retained by the Panzerkorps headquarters and this arrangement may have remained in place until the end of the war.

1.SS-Panzer-Division. The division was withdrawn from the Eastern Front and sent to Belgium where it was rebuilt in April 1944. The division's SS-PzAA 1 was organised according to the November 1943 KstN at this time but on 2 June 1944 all Waffen-SS Panzer divisions were ordered to convert to the April 1944 frei Gliederung establishments, meaning that the reconnaissance battalion was reduced from six to five companies (1). The Allied invasion obviously hampered any attempts at reorganisation but by 12 June SS-PzAA 1 reported that the changes had been made. This unit was one of the few Aufklärungs battalions to operate the Sdkfz 234/2 armoured car and sixteen of these vehicles had been shipped from the Heesezeugamt in late May 1944 and all were concentrated in the Panzerspähzug of the Stabskompanie. This figure was nine short of the authorised number and the other companies were also understrength. The divison took part in the battles of the Normandy campaign, including Operation Lüttich, and lost most of its heavy equipment before small groups of men were able to retreat to the Seine. In October 1944 the division was rebuilt and at that time SS-PzAA 1 was allocated three Sdkfz 234/1 and five Sdkfz 234/3 armoured cars. Somewhat surprisingly, eight Sdkfz 234/2 vehicles were still on hand although less than half of these were considered fully operational.

In December the division took part in the Ardennes Offensive and SS-PzAA 1 was attached to a Kampfgruppe commanded by Sturmbannführer Gustav Knittel which also contained artillery and engineer units. By this time the battalion's heavy company had been disbanded and its assets spread among the remaining companies. The four serviceable Sdkfz 234/2 armoured cars were with 4.Kompanie and 1.Kompanie had no vehicles (2).

In February 1945 the division was transferred to Hungary where it took part in the fighting for the Gran River bridgehead as part of 6.Panzerarmee and Operation Frühlingserwachen, the last major German offensive of the war (3).

Notes

1. This figure includes the Versorgungs-Kompanie. The June order covered the Panzer and Panzergrenadier regiments and also the the Aufklärungs and Panzerjäger battalions. Other units were to be converted as appropriate KstN were issued.

2. Interestingly, a US Army intelligence report which recounted the interrogation of two prisoners from this formation shows that the term Puma was in use at the time, to describe both the Sdkfz 234/1 and 234/2 armoured cars, at least within this battalion.

3 The chart on page 63 of this book shows the battalion's organisation and actual strength July 1944 when the division first went into action on the Normandy front.

2.SS-Panzer-Division. The division was withdrawn from the Eastern Front in stages and transferred to the south of France where, by May 1944, it had been partly rebuilt. The division's SS-PzAA 2 was organised according to the November 1943 guidelines and did not begin its conversion to the April 1944 KstN until the beginning of July. The reorganisation did not entail any immediate increase in the battalion's assets and its new 3.Kompanie was organised as a light reconnaissance company using KstN 1113(gp).

The division took part in the fighting in Normandy, including Operation Lüttich where SS-PzAA 2 formed part of Kampfgruppe Deutschland. On 15 August 1944 three Sdkfz 234/3 armoured cars were shipped to the battalion and on 27 August a total of four Sdkfz 234/1 models were despatched. These vehicles would normally have been assigned to the battalion's Stabskompanie but they are not mentioned in any later reports. At the end of October 1944 the division was withdrawn from the front line and relocated to the area south of Paderborn in Germany to be refurbished. Earlier, on 1 October, two separate shipments saw a total of nine further Sdkfz 234/1 vehicles sent to the battalion but these may not have arrived for some time. Interestingly, a note on the Zuhführungsliste states that this delivery signalled a full allocation and this could only have been correct if the August shipments were still on hand. A report compiled by the division in November 1944 describes the battalion's halftracks by type and number in great detail but states that the Stabskompanie had no armoured cars nor are they listed under the other companies. At least one authoritative source states that the battalion possessed thirteen Sdkfz 234/1 and three Sdkfz 234/3 armoured cars when it took part in the Ardennes Offensive as part of Kampfgruppe Krag.

3.SS-Panzer-Division. The divison's SS-PzAA 3 served on the Eastern Front for its entire existence and throughout 1944 was significantly understrength. On 15 January 1945 the battalion reported that twenty-nine Sdkfz 250 halftracks, six light and four heavy armoured cars were on hand. I can offer no explanation as to what type the latter may be as there is no record of any allocation of Sdkfz 233 armoured cars and the four Sdkfz 234/1 vehicles shipped to the battalion did not leave the Heereszeugamt depot until 31 January.

4.SS-Polizei-Division. See LC 11.

9.SS-Panzer-Division. Formed in mid-1943 the division served on the Eastern Front, in Normandy and famously as part of the force that defended Arnhem in September 1944. From the following month the division was transferred to Germany to be rebuilt and in November 1944 four Sdkfz 234/1 and three Sdkfz 234/3 armoured cars were shipped to SS-PzAA 9 and a further ten Sdkfz 234/1 vehicles were received, due possibly to a simple administrative error which diverted them from 9.Panzer-Division.

The battalion took part in the Ardennes Offensive and the rearguard action that followed the German withdrawal. In early 1945 the division was again rebuilt and sent to Hungary but there was no further allocation of armoured cars. By February 1945 the battalion was so depleted that its two light armoured companies were combined and by the next month the battalion commander reported that just

This evocative image is said to have been made in Silesia in the last weeks of the war as the Wehrmacht fell back further into German territory. Although any positive identification is not possble, the Sdkfz 234/2 armoured car shown here may be from Panzer-Aufklärungs-Abteilung 20.

eleven light and heavy armoured cars, possibly as many as eight of the latter, were on hand together with a number of Sdkfz 250 halftracks. At about this time SS-PzAA 9 was detached from the division and subordinated to 6.Panzer-Division until the end of April 1945.

10.SS-Panzer-Division. The division's SS-PzAA 10 was formed in October 1943 and took part in the battles in Normandy and in the fighting for the Rhine bridge at Arnhem. In December 1944 the battalion was allocated three Sdkfz 234/1 and three Sdkfz 234/3 armoured cars.

The division was held in reserve during the Ardennes Offensive but later took part in Operation Nordwind. In February 1945 the division was transferred to the Eastern Front and was engaged in the defence of Stargard and Fürstenwalde before withdrawing across the Oder River at Stettin, modern-day Szczecin in Poland. In April 1945 the remnants of the division were encircled at Spremberg but managed to escape and head towards Dresden.

During the night of 7 May 1945 the last of the division's armoured vehicles were destroyed by their own crews and although some men were able to reach the West and surrender to the Americans, most were taken into Soviet captivity.

12.SS-Panzer-Division. Formed in late 1943, the division's SS-PzAA 12 was organised according to the November 1943 KstN lists with a Stabkompanie, four reconnaissance companies and a support company. By June 1944 the battalion had been reorganised using the April frei Gliederung KstN establishment and was equipped with Sdkfz 231, Sdkfz 232 and Sdkfz 223 armoured cars and a mixture or Sdkfz 250 and Sdkfz 251 halftracks. Most of these vehicles were lost in the battles in Normandy and at the end of August 1944 the division could only muster 2,500 men and ten tanks. Nevertheless, this small force remained at the front until September when they were finally withdrawn and the division began the process of rebuilding.

In October 1944 SS-PzAA 12 was allocated one Sdkfz 234/1 and three Sdkfz 234/3 armoured cars together with a number of lighter vehicles. In the same month the Stabskompanie was reorganised as a motorised reconnaissance company and the armoured cars were concentrated in 1.Kompanie, which also had a number of halftracks. In November a further three Sdkfz 234/1 models were shipped to SS-PzAA 12 and this gave the battalion its full authorised strength of sixteen Panzerspähwagen.

The division took part in the Ardennes Offensive and in the first week of February 1945 was transferred to the Eastern Front were it was employed in the attempts to destroy the bridgehead the Russians had created on the Gran River north of Esztergom in Hungary. At that time the battalion's 1.Kompanie was converted to an armoured scout company and 3.Kompanie was equipped with VW light cars. The heavy armoured cars which were photographed in Hungary were presumably with the Stabskompanie.

17.SS-Panzergrenadier-Division. See LC 11.

Polizei-Schule-Wein. The police transport training school based in Vienna had a large number of wheeled armoured vehicles on hand including Austrian Steyr ADGZ and Czech Tatra OA vz 30 armoured cars which they referred to respectivel as Polizei-Pzkpfw Steyr and Polizei Pzkpfw-Tatra. In January 1945 a total of ten new Panzerspähwagen were shipped from the Heereszeugamt and although some sources suggest that ten of these were Sdkfz 234/1 armoured cars, the true total is probably five (1). The ad-hoc formation formed from German police units stationed in Vienna was destroyed in the defence of the city.

Fallschirm-Panzer-Division Hermann Göring (HG). The division served on the Italian front until July 1944 when it was transferred to the East, taking part in the fighting around Warsaw. At that time the division's Fallschirm-PzAA-HG contained a staff and five companies, the battalion's 5.Kompanie being a very strong support unit with both 12cm and 8cm mortars. From this it would appear that the battalion was built using the November 1943 KstN but this is far from certain.

In October 1944 the division was in Modlin, north-west of Warsaw, and at that time thirteen Sdkfz 234/1 and three Sdkfz 234/3 armoured cars were shipped to the battalion. In the same month it was renamed Fallschirm-PzAA-HG 1 as a second battalion had been formed for Fallschirm-Panzergrenadier Division 2 (HG). Sometime prior to this, probably in September, the battalion had been reorganised to a four-company establishment.

From January 1945 the division was subordinated to Panzerkorps-Grossdeutschland and supported Panzergrenadier-Division Brandenburg in the fighting around Lodz and conducted a rearguard action to the Oder and Neisse rivers.

In February 1945 Fallschirm-PzAA-HG 1 was reorganised, apparently unofficially, with a headquarters element that contained three armoured companies, numbered 1 to 3, a fourth, armoured company and a fifth company which was equipped with the remaining Sdkfz 234 armoured cars. Although the exact number is unknown the company contained the remaining Sdkfz 234/1 vehicles and three new Sdkfz 234/4 armoured cars which were sent in the same month. A further three Sdkfz 234/4 were dispatched in March and quite possibly another three in April.

Notes

1. The shipment was made up of five 234/1, four Sdkfz 223 or Sdkfz 221 and a single Sdkfz 222.

1
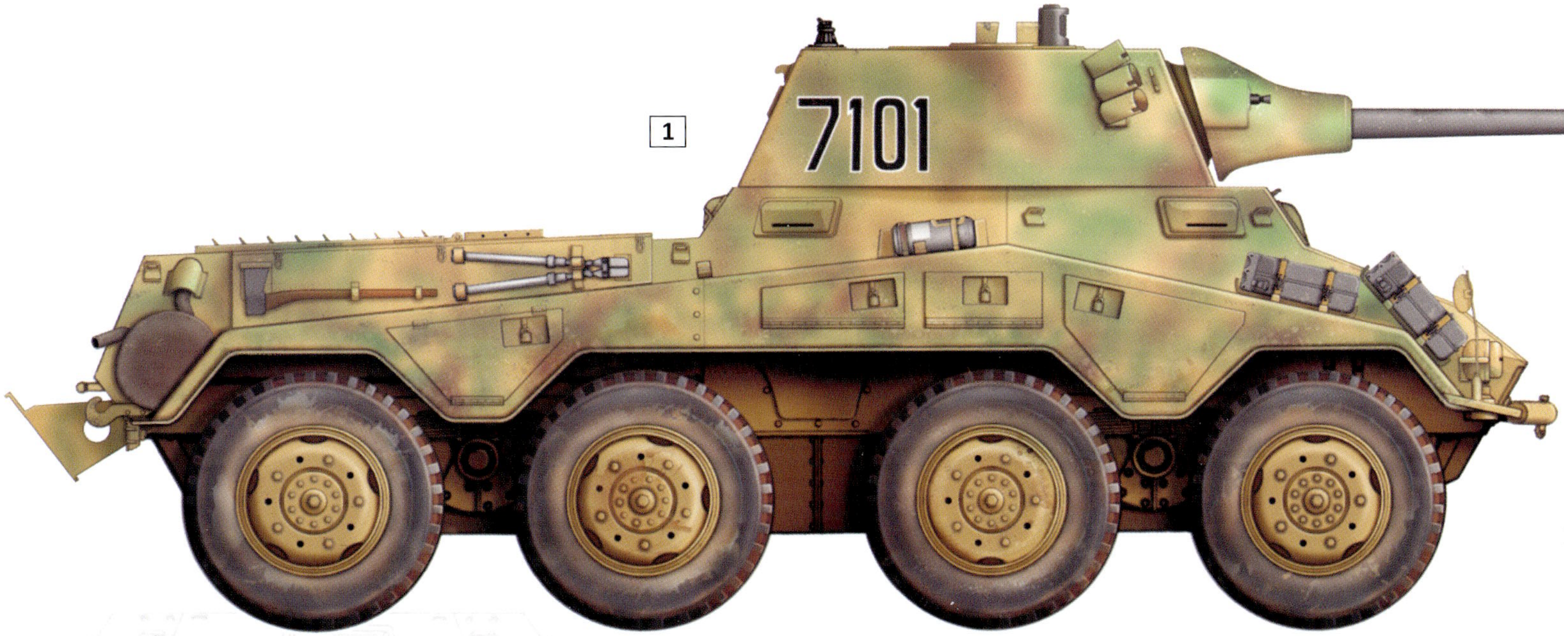

1. Sdkfz 234/2. Unit unknown. Germany, spring 1944. Photographed during a training exercise, the image on which this illustration is based is reproduced on page 64. The turret number is quite unusual but it would seem safe to assume that 7 indicates a troop which suggests a company organised according to KstN 1162a of 1 November 1943. Only the reconnaissance battalions of 2.Panzer-Division and Panzer-Lehr-Division received enough Sdkfz 234/2 armoured cars to equip a full company although neither would seem a likely candidate. Between December 1943 and March 1944 the Aufklärungs-Lehr-Abteilung, based at Krampnitz in Germany, was allocated twenty-six of these vehicles and although most went to Panzer-Lehr-Division some were retained and others were later transferred from the Ersatzheer. It is possible, but speculative at this point, that this was an early numbering system used at Krampnitz until it was superceded by the three-digit numbers seen below (2)

3

4

2
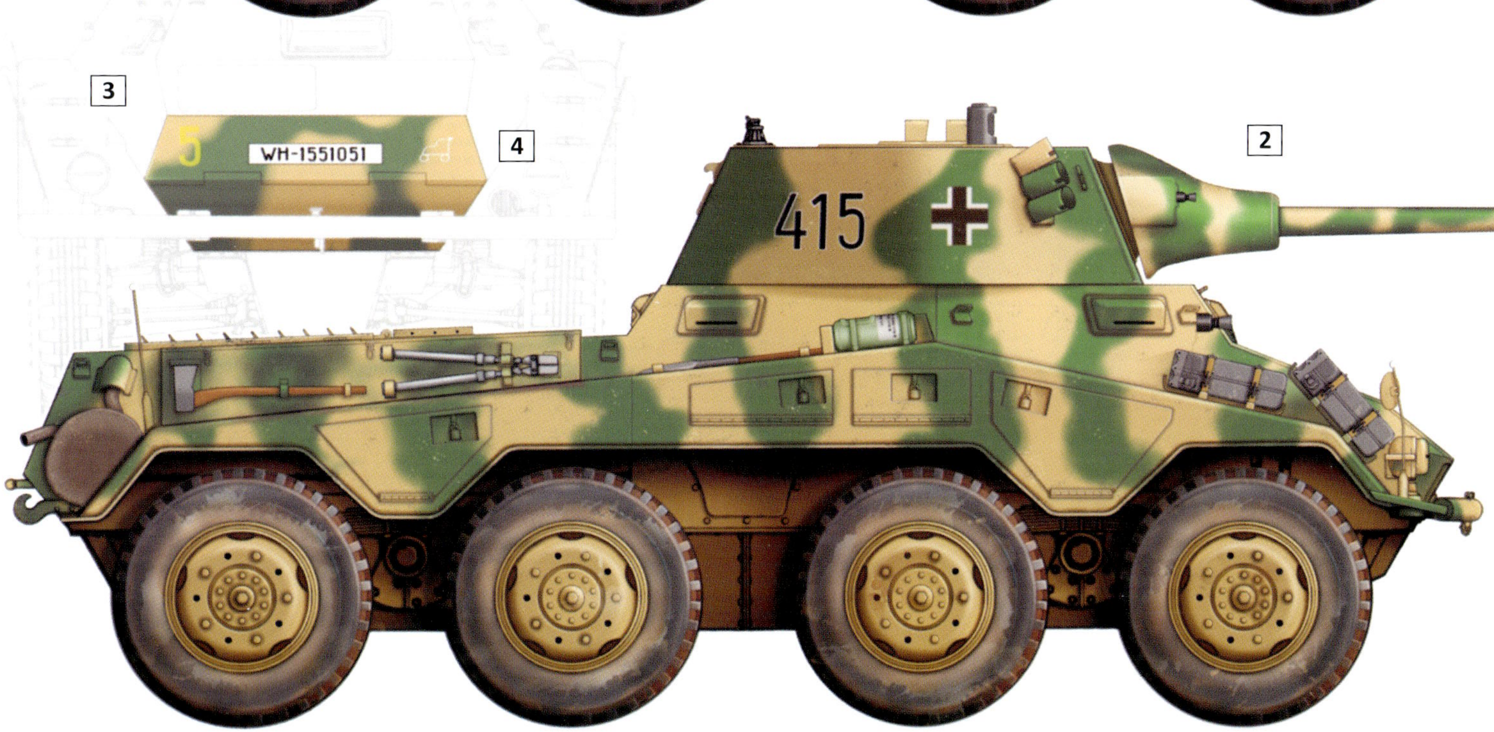

2. Sdkfz 234/2. Unit uncertain. Germany, spring 1944. This vehicle has been associated with a number of units but it was almost certainly assigned to 4.Kompanie, Aufklärungs-Lehr-Abteilung when it was photographed, suggesting that the image was made in early 1944. The individual vehicle number was repeated on the hull front in a light colour, depicted here as yellow (3). Note also the tactical sign denoting an armoured car company (4).

1

1. Sdkfz 234/2. 1.Kompanie, Panzer-Aufklärungs-Abteilung 2. Normandy, summer 1944. The battalion's 1.Kompanie was fully equipped with these armoured cars at the beginning of the Normandy campaign and most, if not all, were camouflaged as this vehicle is with a base of Dunkelgelb, a light mottled application of Olivgrün and bands of Rotbraun. The company was organised by Truppe and the system of turret numbers is explained in detail on page 62.

3

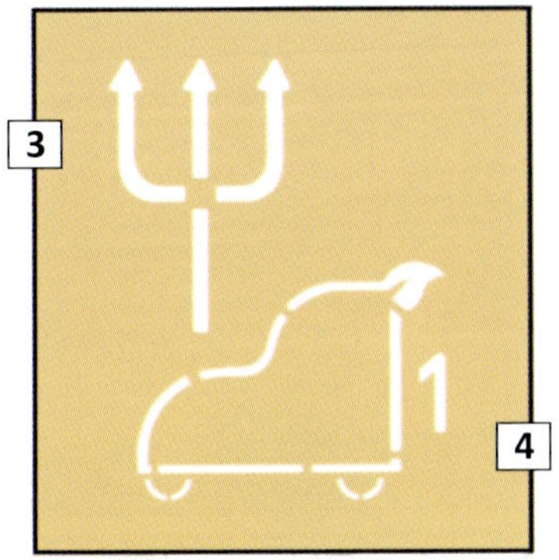

4

2

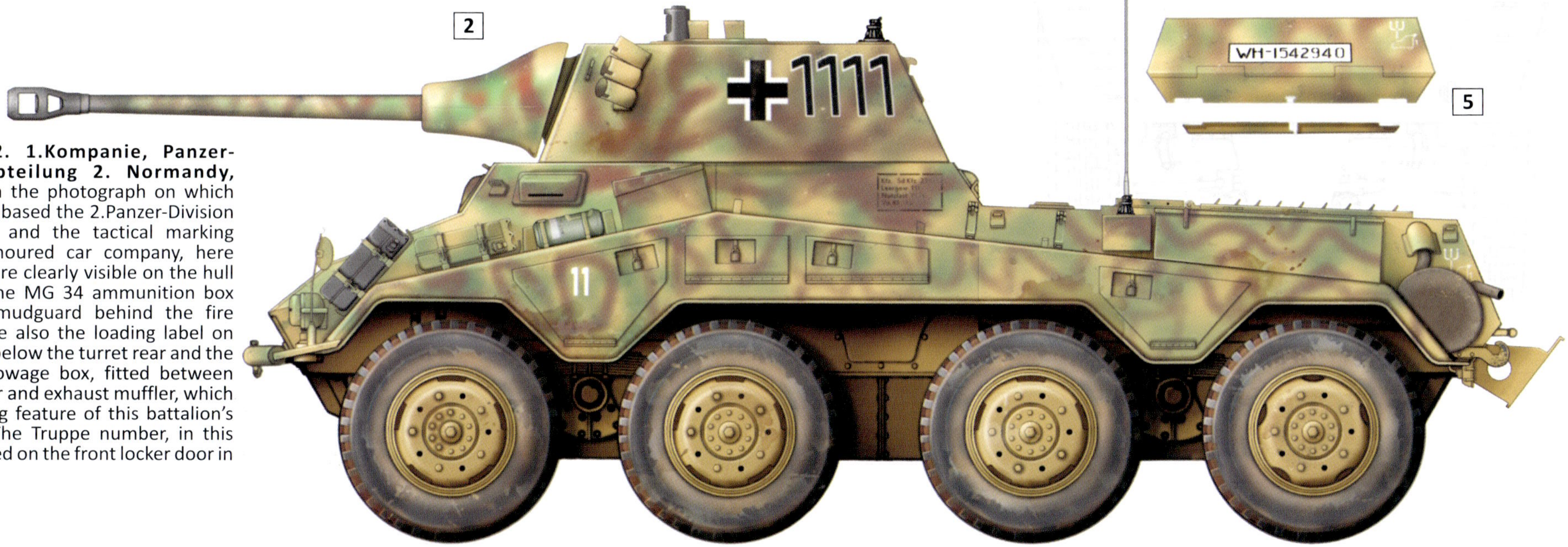

5

2. Sdkfz 234/2. 1.Kompanie, Panzer-Aufklärungs-Abteilung 2. Normandy, summer 1944. In the photograph on which this illustration is based the 2.Panzer-Division unit insignia (3) and the tactical marking denoting an armoured car company, here 1.Kompanie (4), are clearly visible on the hull front (5). Note the MG 34 ammunition box welded to the mudguard behind the fire extinguisher. Note also the loading label on the hull side just below the turret rear and the field-modified stowage box, fitted between the antenna cover and exhaust muffler, which was an identifying feature of this battalion's armoured cars. The Truppe number, in this case 11, is repeated on the front locker door in white.

1

2

4

5

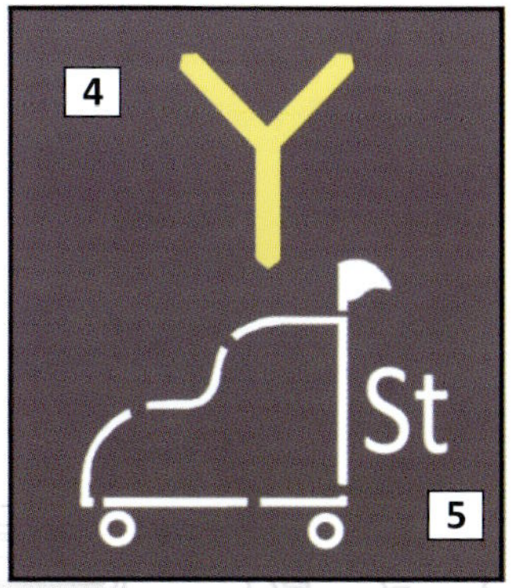

1. Sdkfz 234/2. 1.Kompanie, Panzer-Aufklärungs-Lehr-Abteilung 130. Normandy, summer 1944. A peculiar field modification which could identify armoured cars of this battalion were the small brackets welded to the turret's lower edge, the flash suppressor fitted to the machine gun aperture and the handle fixed to the hull front access door. The Balkenkreuz was carried on the turret rear (2), and possibly the sides, as a black outline only. I have been unable to find a photograph of any of the battalion's armoured cars with a company number.

3

6

3. Sdkfz 234/2. Stab, Panzer-Aufklärungs-Abteilung 7. Lithuania, summer 1944. The battalion received six of these heavy armoured cars in February 1944 and all were initially assigned to 1.Kompanie. By the following July, after some reorganisation, the Sdkfz 234/2 vehicles were all transferred to the Stabskompanie. Photographs show that the 7.Panzer-Division unit insignia (4) and tactical sign identifying the headquarters of a reconnaissance battalion (5) were carried on the hull front on a dark background, possibly black or dark grey, as shown here (6). This vehicle is painted in the standard base coat of Dunkelgelb with randomly applied patches of Rotbraun and Olivgrün.

1

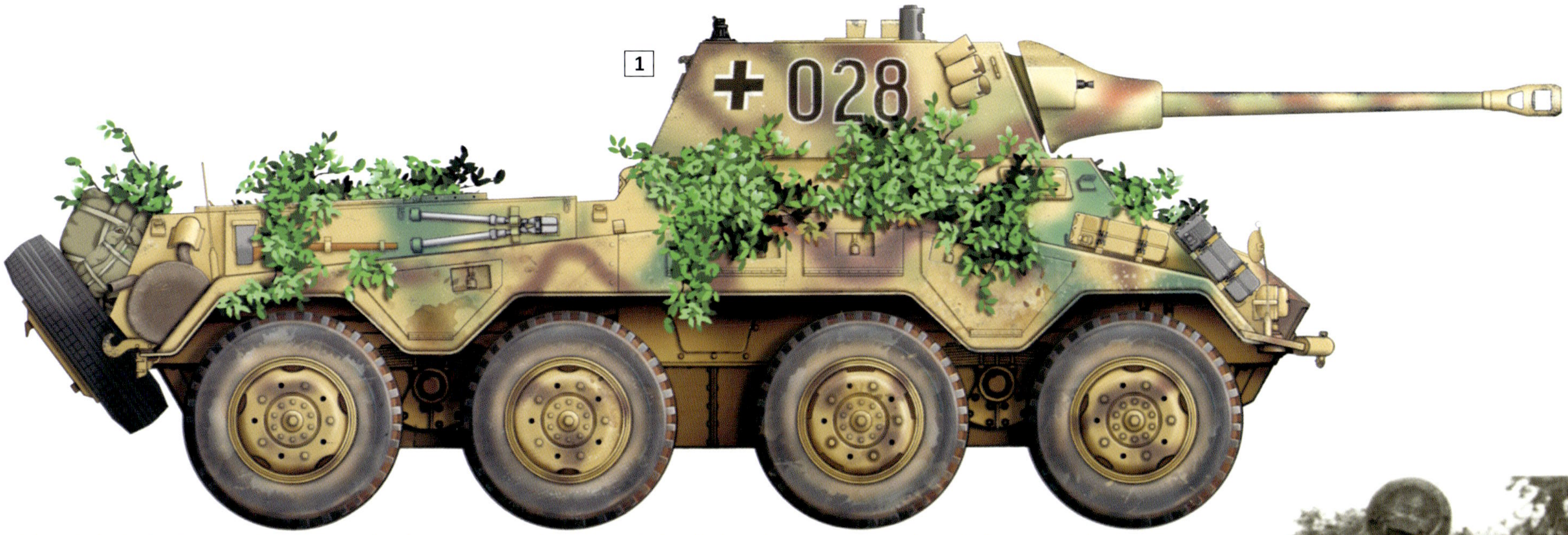

1. Sdkfz 234/2. Stab, SS-Panzer-Aufklärungs-Abteilung 1. Normandy, summer 1944. The battalion never received its full allocation of these vehicles and the sixteen that did arrive were detached as part of an ad-hoc unit and fought most of the Normandy battles with 12.SS-Panzer-Division. The exact significance of the numbering system is not known and a possible explanation is provided on page 63. The camouflage pattern, made up of a soft mottling of Olivgrün and wavy lines of Rotbraun, would seem to have been common, if not universal.

3

2

2. Sdkfz 234/2. Panzer-Aufklärungs-Lehr-Abteilung 130. France, autumn 1944. The rather complicated history of this vehicle is discussed in the photo captions on pages 5 and 9. The modifications to the turret and hull, as described on the previous page and also visible in our photograph (3), identify this armoured car as one of the battalion's Normandy survivors but the turret number suggests that the remaining Sdkfz 234/2 vehicles were now assigned to 4.Kompanie. Under the KstN establishments of August 1944 the battalion's fourth, or heavy, company was made up of Teileinheiten, that is parts of units, and it may have seemed appropriate to place the heavy armoured cars there.

1. Sdkfz 234/2. Panzer-Aufklärungs-Abteilung 2. Belgium, winter 1944. Photographed at some time after the conclusion of the Ardennes Offensive, this vehicle of Kampfgruppe von Böhm was transported to the United States and was later revealed to be the Sdkfz 234/2 armoured car of Panzer-Aufklärungs-Lehr-Abteilung 130 shown on the previous page and in or photograph (2). Note the small brackets on the turret sides and the handle on the hull access door and the complete absence of any markings.

1

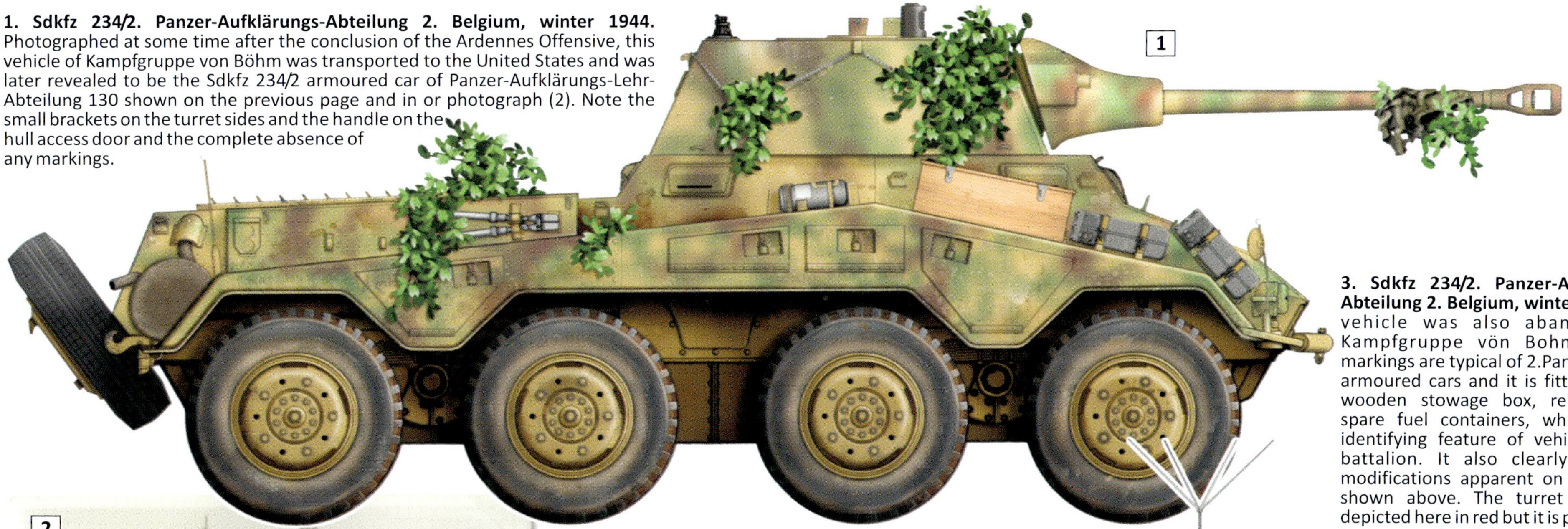

2

2. Our photograph shows the vehicle of Panzer-Aufklärungs-Abteilung 2 captured in Belgium after it had been exposed to the elements for almost two years. The turret number 432 is clearly visible as is the Balkenkreuz, neither of which could be seen in December 1944. Note also the distinctive handle on the hull access door (A) and the small brackets (B) on the turret sides.

3. Sdkfz 234/2. Panzer-Aufklärungs-Abteilung 2. Belgium, winter 1944. This vehicle was also abandoned by Kampfgruppe vön Bohm but the markings are typical of 2.Panzer-Division armoured cars and it is fitted with the wooden stowage box, replacing the spare fuel containers, which was an identifying feature of vehicles of this battalion. It also clearly lacks the modifications apparent on the vehicle shown above. The turret number is depicted here in red but it is possible that it was rendered in some other dark colour as is sometimes suggested. Note the Truppe number painted on the forward locker door of the mudguard, a system which the battalion had used since Normandy. A photograph of this vehicle is reproduced on page 10.

3

1

1. Sdkfz 234/2. Stabskompanie, Panzer-Aufklärungs-Abteilung 7. East Prussia, late 1944 or early 1945. The identification with this battalion was based on a study of vehicle registration numbers from available photographs and was suggested by German researcher Martin Block. Although parts of this vehicle were heavily damaged, especially the turret roof, enough was visible in our photograph, reproduced on page 6, to render an accurate representation of the camouflage pattern.

2

3

2. Sdkfz 234/2. Stabskompanie, Panzer-Aufklärungs-Abteilung 20. East Prussia, early 1945. The battalion received sixteen of these armoured cars in June 1944 and reported that ten were still on hand in April 1945. They served throughout with the battalion's Stabskompanie and all appear to have carried turret numbers beginning with 0, probably followed by the Zug, here 4, and individual vehicle. Note that the position changes on the right side (3). Other examples are shown on page 25

1

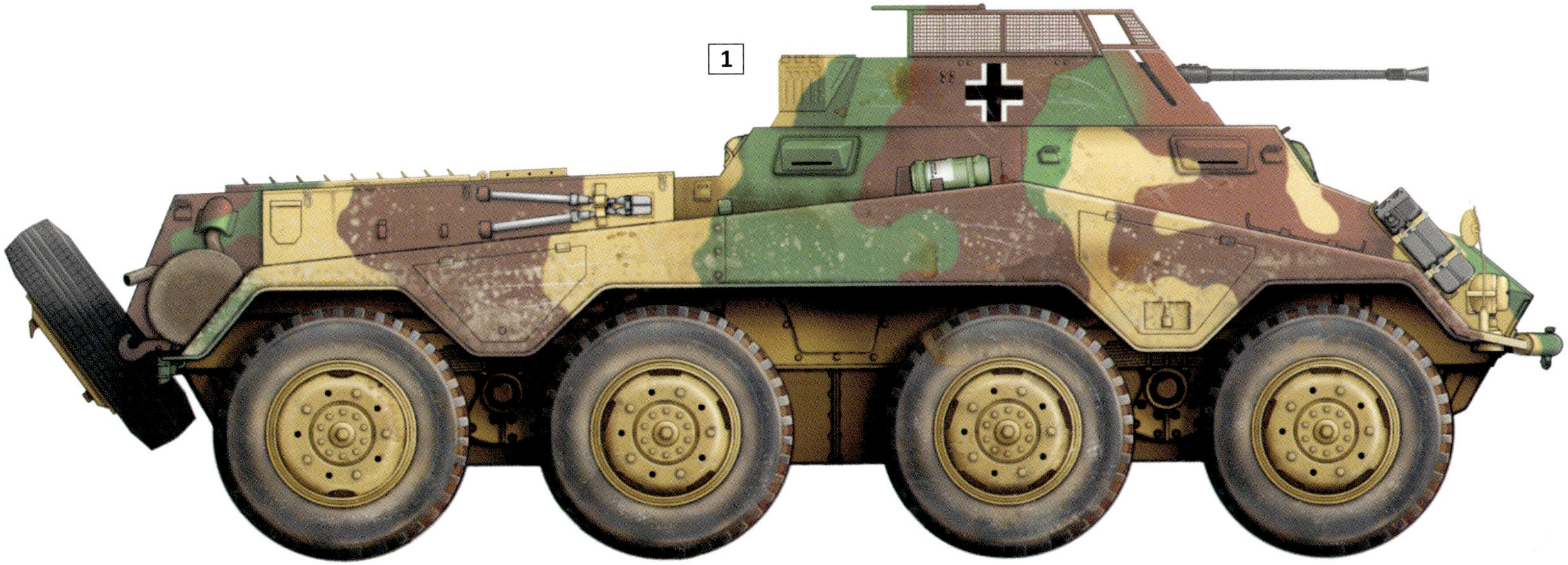

2

4

1. Sdkfz 234/1. Stabskompanie, Panzer-Aufklärungs-Abteilung 125. Germany, spring 1945. From late October 1944, and possibly earlier, camouflage was applied to armoured vehicles before they left the factories. As explained in the Technical Details and Modifications section, this process may not have been instituted with the Sdkfz 234 series of armoured cars until December and the pattern shown here I have classified, purely as a matter of convenience, as Type I. The contours of the darker colours are quite clear in the photograph on which this illustration is based and Rotbraun appears to dominate. The wheel hubs were sometimes painted but this does not seem to be the case here. The unit insignia of 25.Panzergrenadier-Division (2), this battalion's parent formation, is not visible in our photograph but may have been present.

3

5

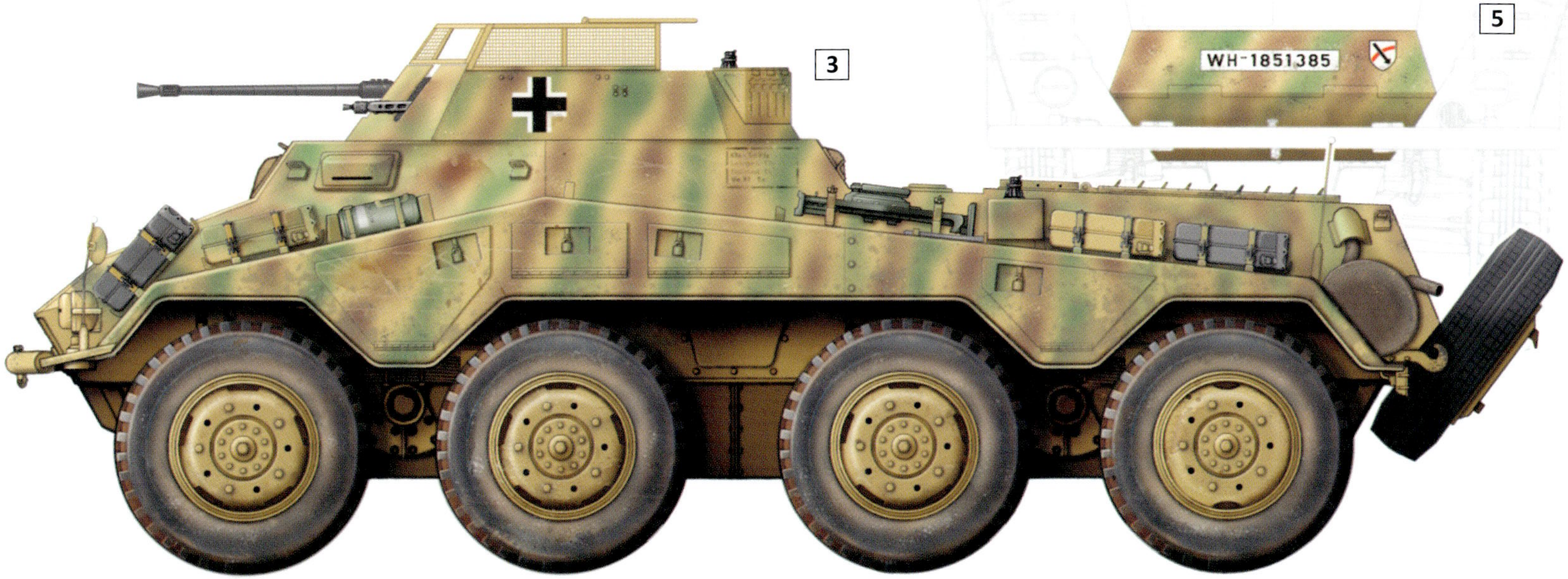

3. Sdkfz 234/1. Stabskompanie, Panzer-Aufklärungs-Abteilung 6. Austria, spring 1945. The battalion was assigned thirteen of these armoured cars and while it is unclear how many were on hand in the last weeks of the war, this vehicle must be one of the original allocations made in August and September 1944. A variation of the 6.Panzer-Division unit insignia (4) is clearly visible in the photograph used to create this illustration on the hull front (5), as is the vehicle registration number.

1 and 2. Sdkfz 234/1. Panzer-Aufklärungs-Abteilung 4. Danzig, early 1945. The battalion was allocated as many as seven of these armoured cars in January 1945 and they probably arrived in the following month. The vehicle depicted here was photographed extensively, allowing an accurate representation of the factory-applied camouflage scheme. It is a perhaps a later variant of the pattern shown on the previous page and I have termed it, for the purposes of this book, as Type II. The proportion of Olivgrün has increased and the shapes are simplified.

1

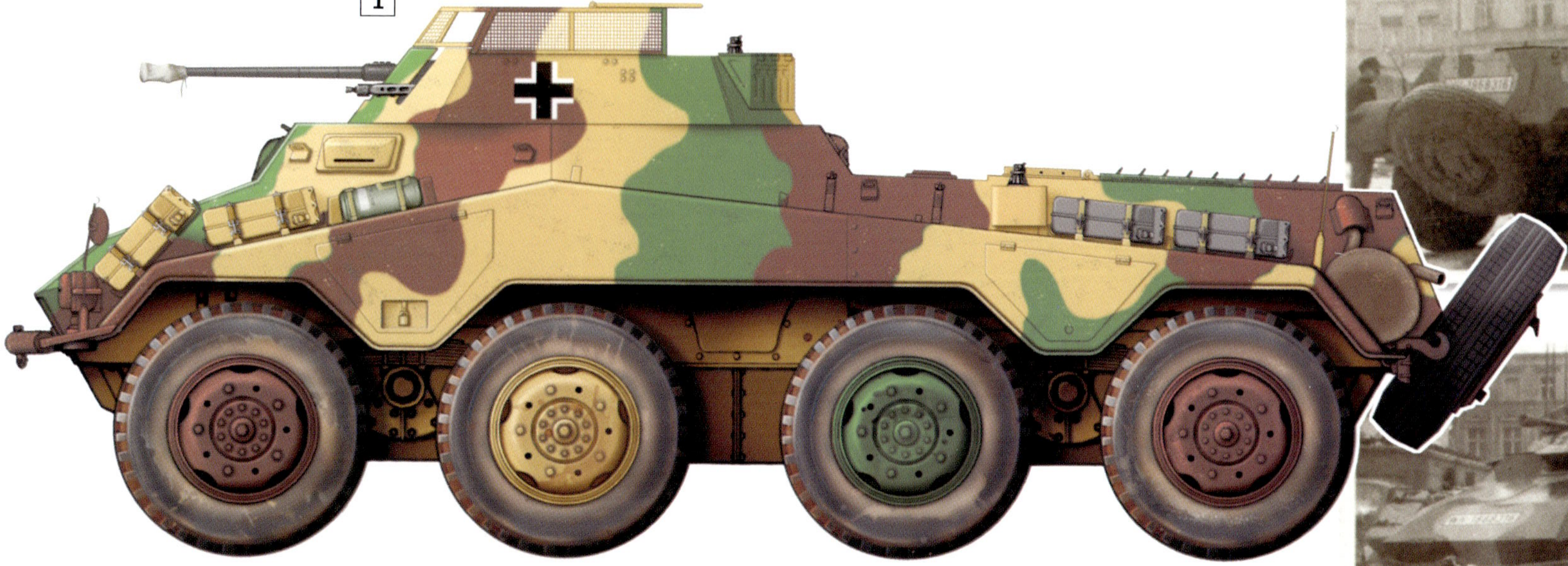

3

4

This pattern is the most commonly seen on Sdkfz 234/4 models, although the wheels were usually left unpainted, which was the only other version still in production. Our photographs (3 and 4) clearly show that registration numbers were applied to the front and rear hull but there is no unit insignia, suggesting that these images were made shortly after the vehicle arrived.

2

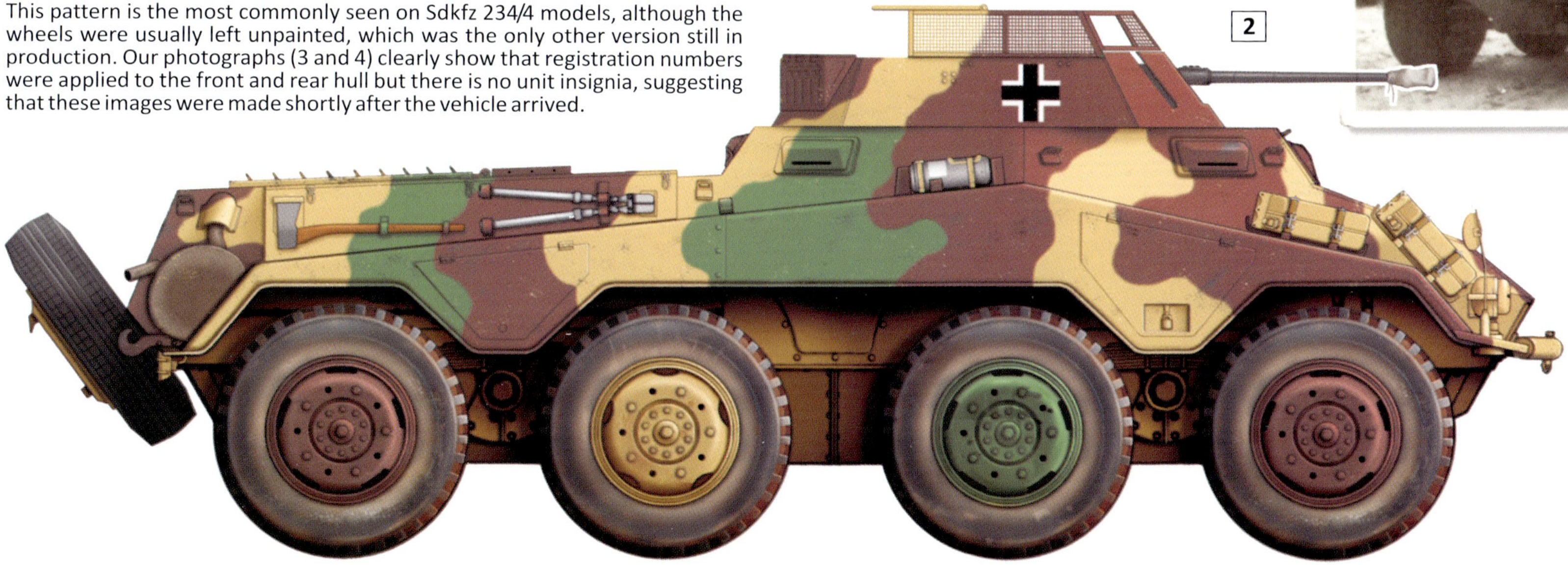

1

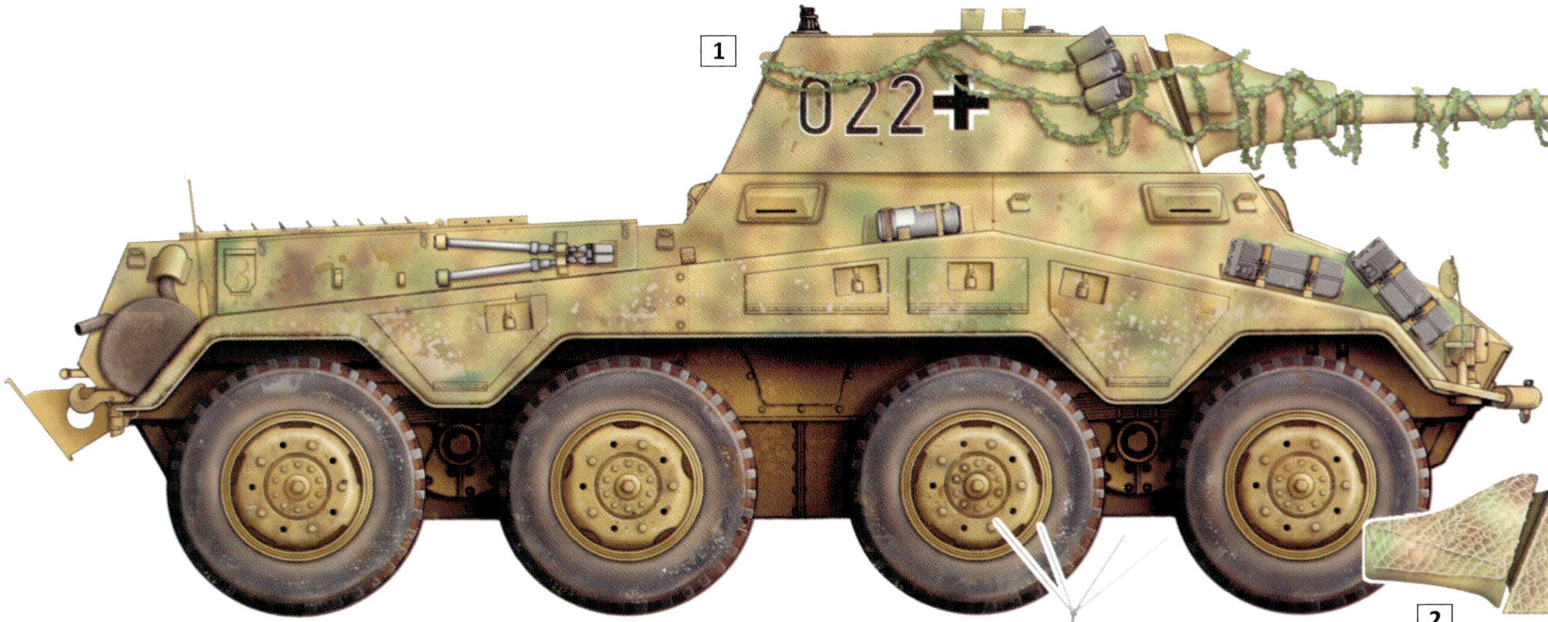

4

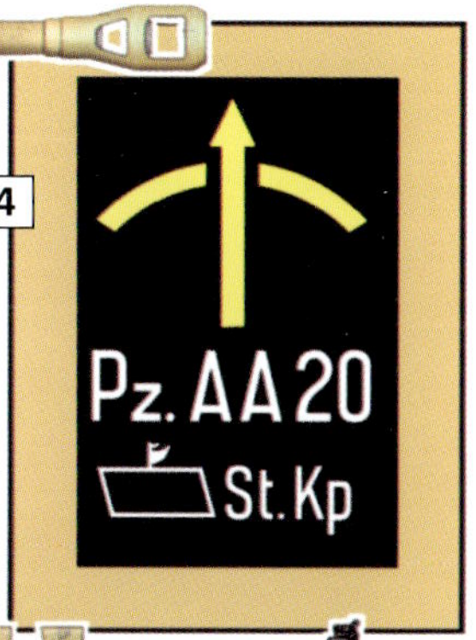

2

3

1. Sdkfz 234/2. Stabskompanie, Panzer-Aufklärungs-Abteilung 20. Czechoslovakia, spring 1945. Photographed at a vehicle dump near Pilsen, this armoured car appeared to be in complete working order except for the tyres which were flat. As mentioned on page 22 these vehicles were all numbered starting with 0. The remnants of the battalion surrendered to units of the US Army in northern Czechoslovakia and other vehicles filmed at the time (2 and 3) show how the style of number could vary. Photographs show that the combined 20.Panzer-Division unit insignia, title and tactical sign (4) was carried by some vehicles on the hull front and rear.

5

5. Sdkfz 234/1. Unit uncertain. Czechoslovakia, spring 1945. The photograph on which this illustration is based is reproduced on page 12 and the location has been confirmed as Chvalsiny in the present-day Czech Republic. Although it is difficult to ascertain the position of any unit at this stage of the war, the reconnaissance battalions of Panzerkorps-Feldherrnhalle and 25.Panzer-Division, both of which had numbers of these armoured cars, withdrew through this area in April 1945. Note the missing locker doors, a common occurrence, which reveals the primer colour inside. The latter also seems to have been used on the turret's protective screen.

1. Sdkfz 234/1. Unit unknown. Germany, spring 1945. Said to have been abandoned after the fighting along the Elbe river in the last days of the war, the photograph which was used to create this illustration is shown on page 11. Although this vehicle is fitted with the simplified mudguards which may have been introduced in December 1944 it is not painted in one of the factory-applied camouflage schemes which were common by this time.

1

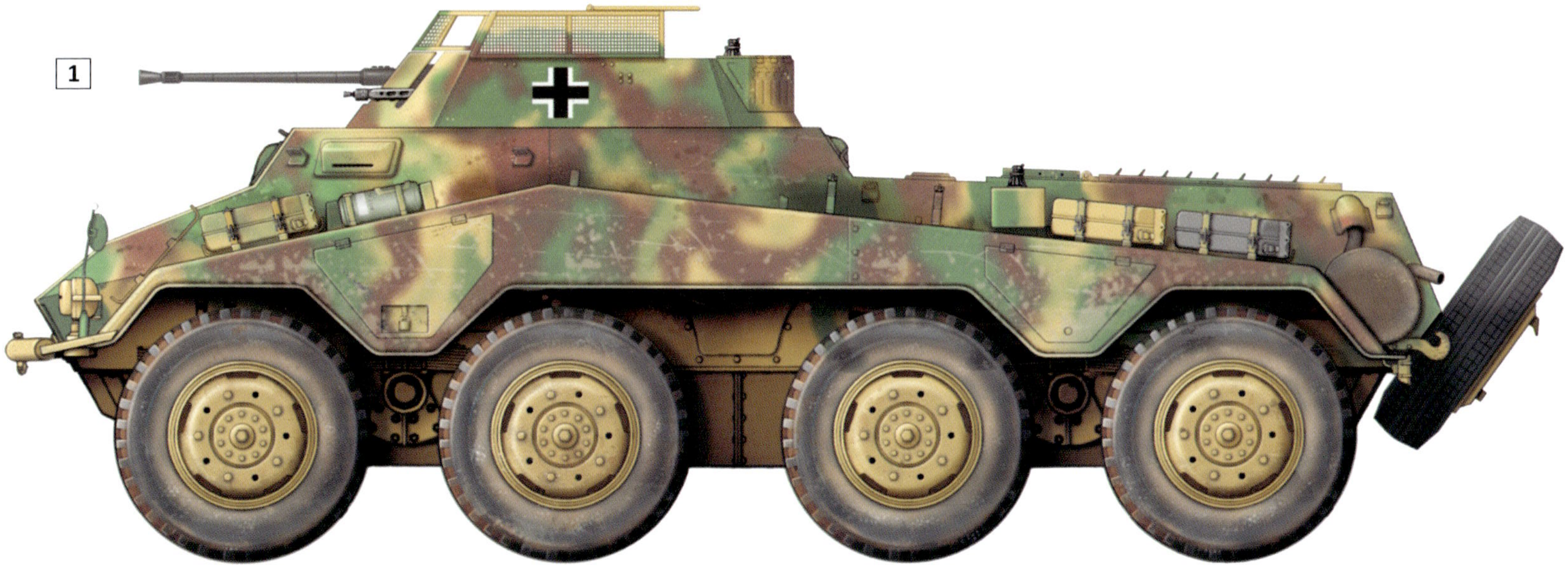

4

2. Sdkfz 234/2 field conversion. Unit unknown. Czechoslovakia, spring 1945. This curious vehicle was created by adding the turret of a Pzkfw II ausf L, the so-called Luchs, to the hull of an Sdkfz 234/2 armoured car, presumably after one or both were damaged. Although any attempt at identification can only be speculative at this time a possible connection to Panzer-Aufklärungs-Abteilung 17 is explained in the unit histories. Similarly, the camouflage pattern is largely guesswork as just one photograph, taken from the front, was made of this vehicle. Note that a portion of the hull front has been painted over (3) and it is tempting to think that this may have been to eradicate some kind of marking. As a matter of interest I have shown the combined 17.Panzer-Division unit insignia and tactical sign (4) known to have been used by Panzer-Aufklärungs-Abteilung 17 towards the end of the war.

2

3

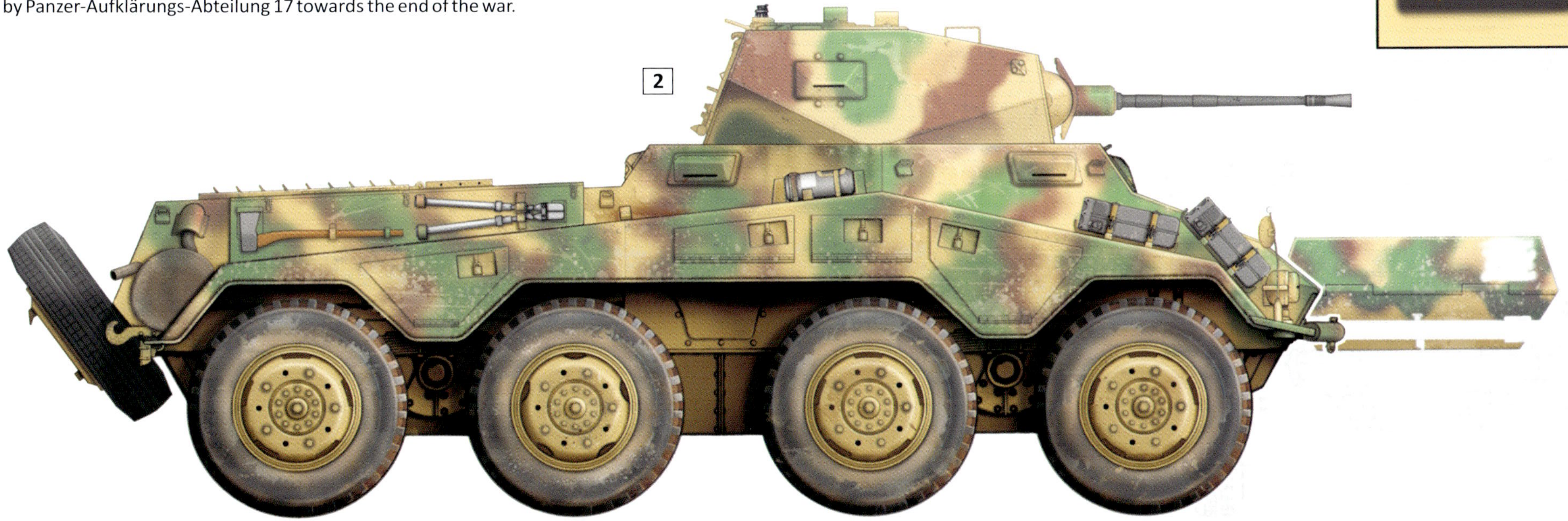

SDKFZ 234/2

1/76 SCALE

THEODOROS KALAMATAS

Theodoros' model is based on the 1/76 scale Matchbox kit that has been on the market in one form or another since 1978. Long out of production it was re-released under the Revell logo in 2005 complete with scenic base which was a feature of Matchbox's armour kits. The model's diminutive size is amply illustrated in the photograph below.

Theodoros has managed to acquire the complete Matchbox 1/76 scale collection and expects to have them all built and painted to this standard. To achieve the effects seen here he uses Tamiya acrylics and a number of different weathering products from Ammo by MIG and AK Interactive. The subtle depiction of the camouflage is impressive, particularly in this small scale. The finished model was built straight from the box without any improvements or alterations.

SDKFZ 234/1

1/35 SCALE

CARLOS MARTIN

Carlos used Tamiya's 1/35 scale Sdkfz 234/1 kit, shown above, which in addition to the armoured car contains three figures, a DKW NZ 350 motorcycle and an assortment of machine guns, pistols, gas mask canisters, bags, water bottles and other items.

Below, left: The motorcyle rider and one of the armoured car crewmen assembled and ready for painting. Below, right: The DKW NZ 350 motorcycle with added brake and clutch cables.

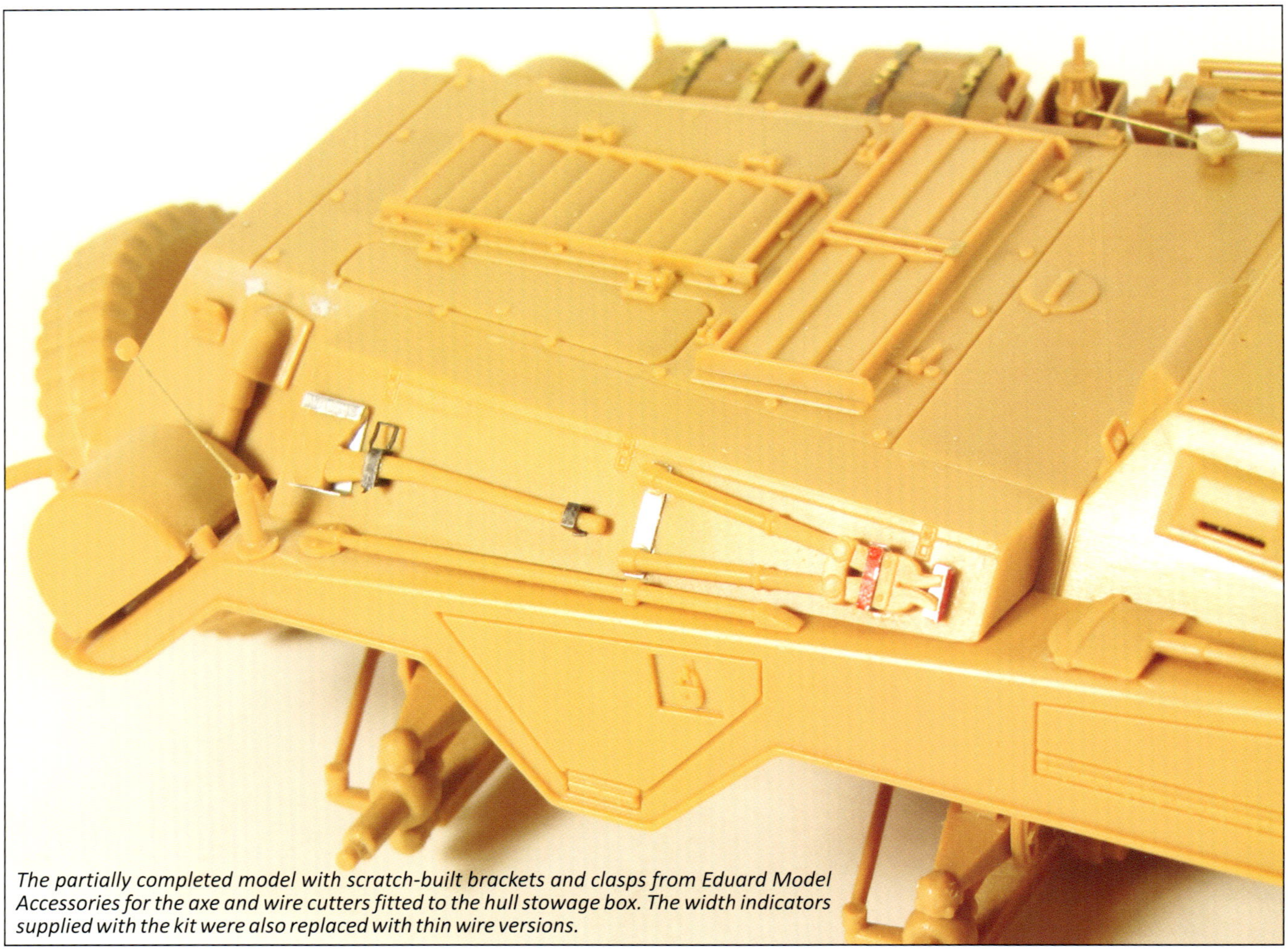

The partially completed model with scratch-built brackets and clasps from Eduard Model Accessories for the axe and wire cutters fitted to the hull stowage box. The width indicators supplied with the kit were also replaced with thin wire versions.

Carlos added the antenna cable and the wrench, made from white plastic rod, and thinned the racks for the fuel containers.

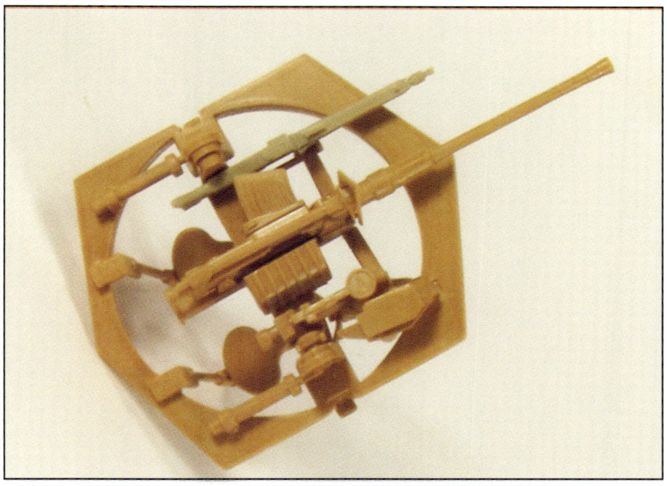

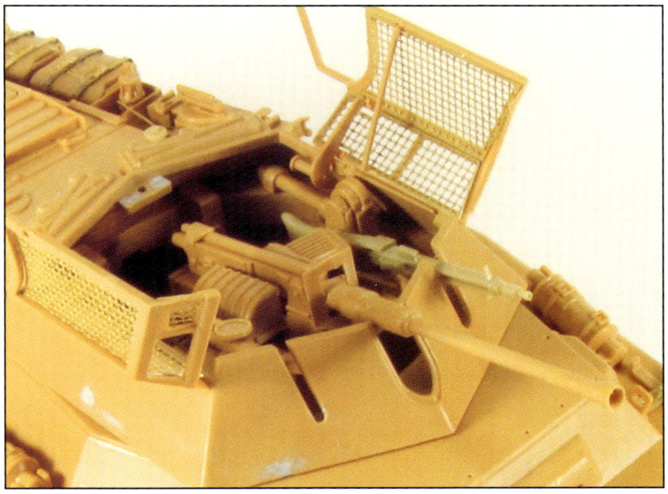

Below: The fully-assembled model. Above: Details of the Hängelafette 38 turret. Although Carlos built this with the parts supplied in the kit many were reworked to a more correct scale size. The photo-etched brass screen is included with the model.

Carlos' completed model finished in a plain base coat of Dunkelgelb RAL 7028. The weathering, particularly the mud accumulated on the wheels, is extremely realistic. Shown below are: 1. The interior of the turret with 2cm gun and MG 42. 2. The fuel containers and the brackets used to hold them in place. 3. The hull radio antenna insulator and its protective cover, the jack and long-handled shovel. 4. One of the ammunition storage containers on the turret rear.

Two views of the completed model. Carlos' finishing technique, although uncomplicated, is exceptionally effective and employs Tamiya acrylic paints and weathering products from AK Interactive.

SDKFZ 234/1

1/35 SCALE

JOHANNES PAMBUDI UTOMO

Johannes' model is based on the Italeri Sdkfz 234/1 1/35 scale kit which was first released in 1996. Some parts, notably the interior details of the Hängelafette 38 turret, were taken from the Dragon Models' Sdkfz 234/1 while other details, such as the turret's protective screen, were scratch-built. The crew figures are from Academy's Tiger I but the poses were drastically altered.

Once built, Johannes painted the model with products from the Arte Deco range by Acylicos Vallego and treated it with weathering pigments from AK Interactive.

The scenic base was made from rocks and pebbles of various sizes and fine soil. The leaves which make up the foliage camouflage were cut from thin paper and applied individually. The long grass is made from human hair painted with Tamiya acrylics.

SDKFZ 234/1

1/35 SCALE

THEODOSIS
GIANNAKIDIS

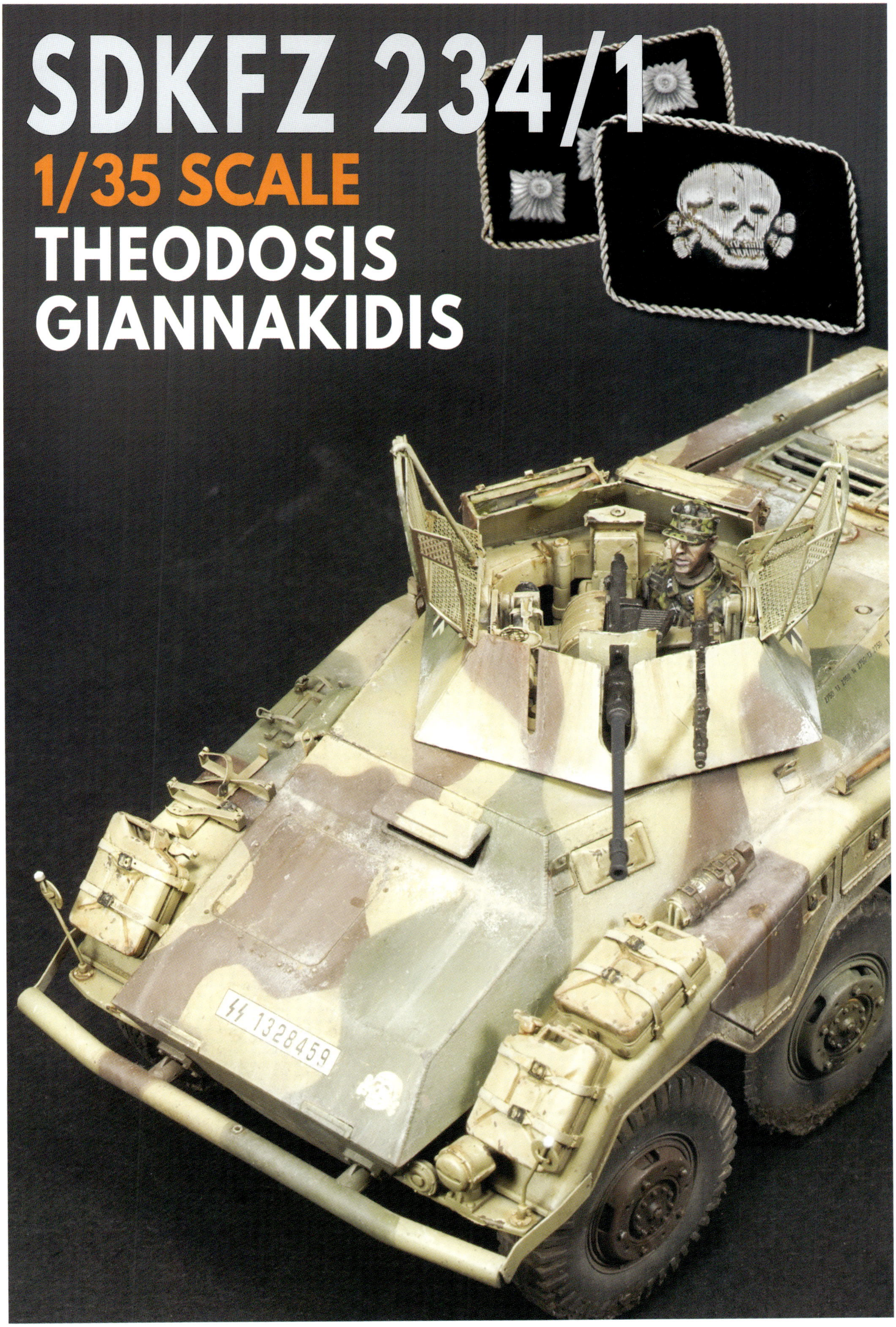

Theodosis' replica is based on the Dragon Models' Sd.Kfz.234/1 Schwerer Panzerspähwagen (2cm) Premium Edition 1/35 scale kit, shown at right. This model was first released in 2019 and contained new parts and was based on the 2006 Sdkfz 234/4 kit.

Shown below are the Aber photo-etched brass details for the Hängelafette 38 turret, rear view mirrors and fuel containers racks.

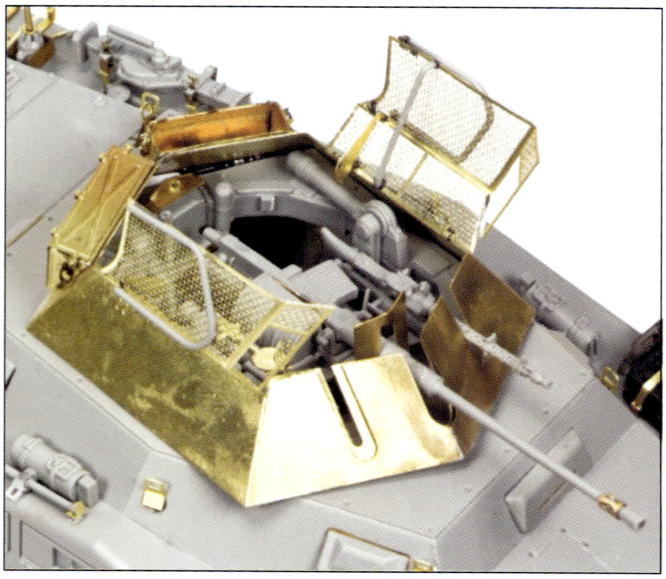

The partly assembled model painted in the factory-applied scheme of Dunkelgelb, Olivgrün and Rotbraun. Theodosis used the 1945 Panzer Colors set from AK Interactive.

The completed model on its scenic base. The vehicle was weathered with Vallejo Pigments Rust, Dark Red Ochre and New Rust. Washes were applied with AK Interactive Crusted Rust Deposits and Light Rust mixed with artist's oils.

At left: The finished model complete with crewman and painted to depict a vehicle of SS-Panzer-Aufklarungs-Abteilung 3. The battalion was allocated four of these heavy armoured cars in late January 1945. Below; The interior of the Hängelafette 38 turret showing details of the 2cm gun and MG 34.

As the first title in this series examined the Sdkfz 234/3 and Sdkfz 234/4 heavy armoured cars I have tried to concentrate here on the versions covered by this book, the Sdkfz 234/1 and 234/2 models. In addition, I have limited this section of the book to the major manufacturers and the accessory producers, of which there are scores, to those of which I have personal knowledge and increased the size of the Model Showcase chapter. I am sure that most readers will agree that armoured cars and halftracks are not as popular as the larger fighting vehicles, such as the Tiger and Panther, and this is reflected in the options available. Still, when one considers just how few production vehicles in the Sdkfz 234 series were assembled and assigned to operational units, the number of products on offer is quite significant and caters for modellers and wargamers alike. An index of manufacturers, with their contact details, can be found on page 64.

DRAGON MODELS LIMITED

Dragon Models was one of the first of the major manufacturers to offer accurate replicas in 1/35 scale and their kits are today something of a benchmark. The company's small scale releases are some of the best available. At the time of writing this Hong Kong-based company offered scale replicas of all four Sdkfz 234 versions and also the experimental 7.5cm L48 mounting. The 2cm Schwebelafette conversion was released under the Cyberhobby label.

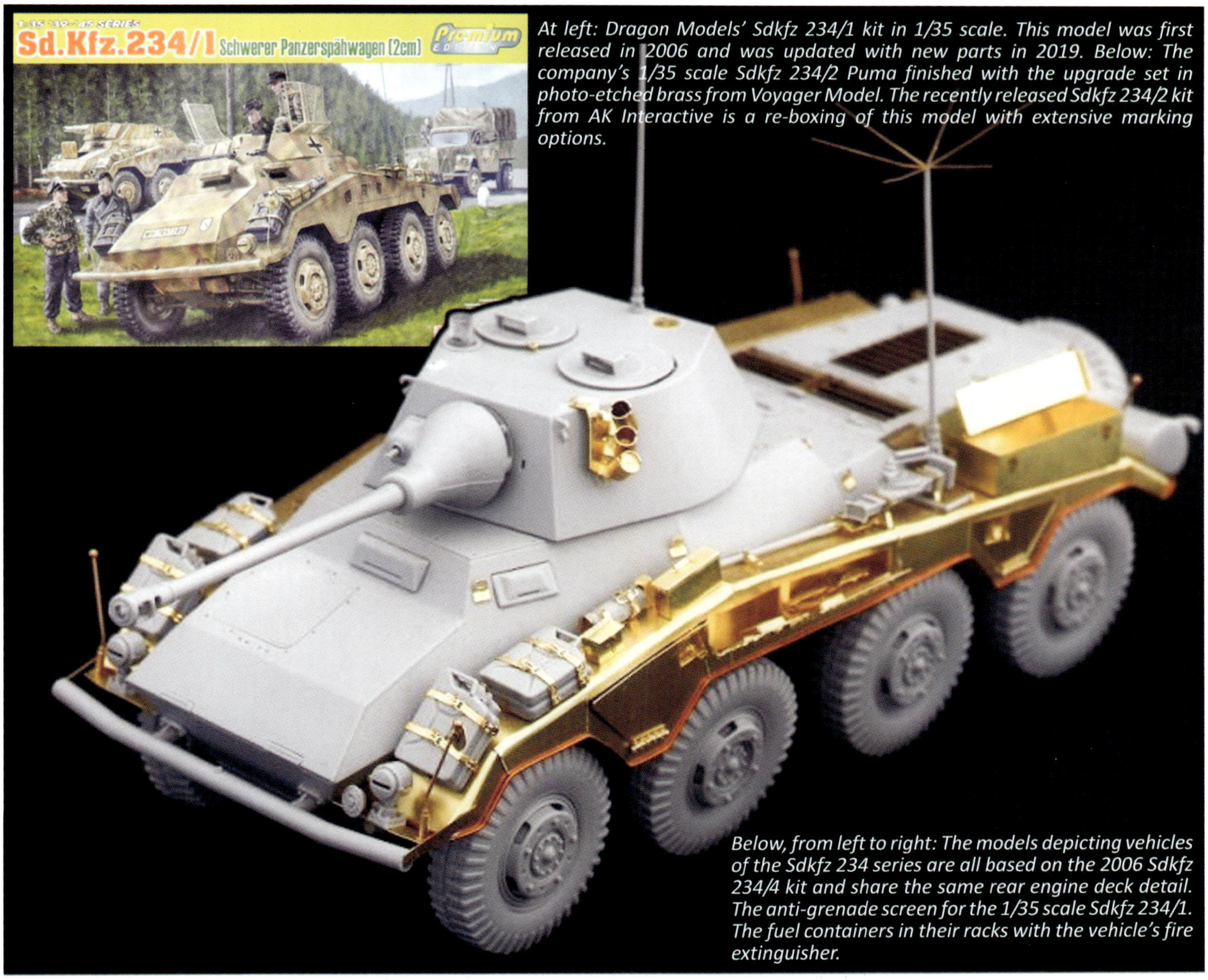

At left: Dragon Models' Sdkfz 234/1 kit in 1/35 scale. This model was first released in 2006 and was updated with new parts in 2019. Below: The company's 1/35 scale Sdkfz 234/2 Puma finished with the upgrade set in photo-etched brass from Voyager Model. The recently released Sdkfz 234/2 kit from AK Interactive is a re-boxing of this model with extensive marking options.

Below, from left to right: The models depicting vehicles of the Sdkfz 234 series are all based on the 2006 Sdkfz 234/4 kit and share the same rear engine deck detail. The anti-grenade screen for the 1/35 scale Sdkfz 234/1. The fuel containers in their racks with the vehicle's fire extinguisher.

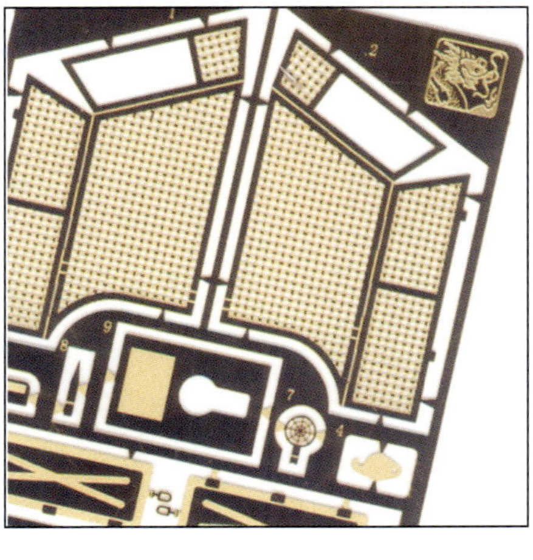

TAMIYA INC

This Japanese company is currently the largest producer of scale model kits in the world, releasing their first armoured vehicle kit in 1961. The company's near monopoly of the 1/35 scale market remained unchallenged until the release of the first Dragon Models' kits in 1987. The company's Sdkfz 234/3 model in 1/35 scale was in fact a re-boxing of the Italeri model, with Tamiya figures included, and although it seems to have been dropped from the catalogue it is still available from some retailers. The Sdkfz 234/2 was first released in 2004 and has supplied many parts for a reworked version that was first offered in 2015 and an Sdkfz 234/1 which was released in the same year. The sole 1/48 scale offering at the time of writing is an Sdkfz 234/2 armoured car.

At left: Tamiya's 1/48 scale Sdkfz 234/2. Unfortunately this attractive kit seems to have been deleted from the company's catalogue. Below: The 1/35 scale Sdkfz 234/1 with crew figures including the motorcycle rider.

Below, from left to right: The interior of the 1/35 scale Sdkfz 234/1 model. The mudguard, headlight, fuel containers and fire extinguisher of the Sdkfz 234/2, aslo in 1/35 scale. Detail of the Sdkfz 234/1 kit shown above.

ATTACK HOBBY KITS

Also known as Attack HK, this Czech company specialises in replicas of military vehicles of the Second World War period, particulary the less well known types, all in 1/72 scale. The current catalogue offers an Sdkfz 234/2 armoured car and the field-modified conversion of an Sdkfz 234/2 fitted with a Pzkpfw II ausf L turret, of which just one was built.

At left: The Attack Hobby Kits' Sdkfz 234/2 conversion fitted with a Pzkpfw II turret in 1/72 scale. The company markets this model as the Puchs, that is a combination of the terms Puma and Luchs. This unique vehicle is also shown and discussed in the Camouflage & Markings section on page 26 of this book. Above: The detailed turret which is included in the latest version of the company's Sdkfz 234/2 Puma kit.

HASEGAWA

This Japanese company offers an Sdkfz 234/1, Sdkfz 234/2 and Sdkfz 234/3 in 1/72 scale. While some of this manufacturer's early kits were quite basic, sometimes these models are accurate and well detailed. All have extensive marking options and some interior details. Dan Taylor Modelworks produces a very nice anti-grenade screen for the Sdkfz 234/1.

Above: Hasegawa's Sdkfz 234/3 and Sdkfz 234/1 kits, both in 1/72 scale. Left: The Hasegawa 1/72 scale Sdkfz 234/2 assembled and completed with the photo-etched brass detail set from Eduard Model Accessories. Below: The photo-etched brass anti-grenade screen from Dan Taylor Modelworks mentioned above.

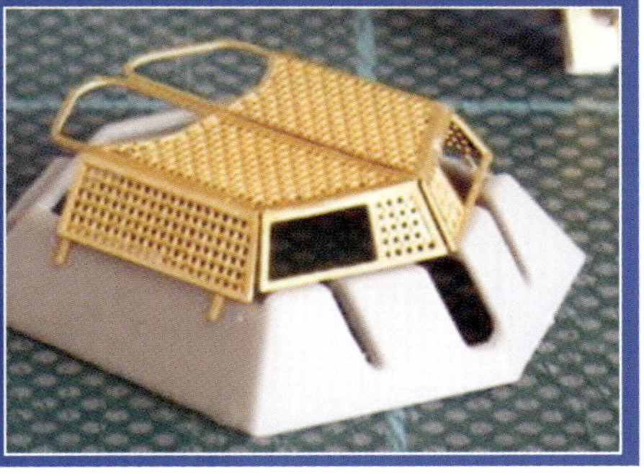

AIRFIX, MATCHBOX AND REVELL

No list of scale model armoured cars would be complete without at least some mention of the venerable Airfix Sdkfz 234 kit. First released in 1964, this model has been repackaged and rereleased many times including as part of a boxed set in the company's Battlefront History Series which also included the Pzkfw IV kit and a number of plastic figures. Its inaccuracies are well known and although conversion sets are available they are rather crude and expensive. The Sdkfz 234/2 currently on offer from Revell, shown below, is the old Matchbox kit first released in 1978 complete with scenic base, for which the company was famous.

At left: The original packaging of the Matchbox Sdkfz 234/2 kit. The company's moulds were acquired by Revell in the early 1990s and select items are released from time to time.

ITALERI

In the popular 1/35 scale this Italian company has released models of all four production versions of the Sdkfz 234 series. In addition, there are also 1/72 scale models of the same vehicles and an Sdkfz 234/2 in 1/56 scale with the promise of more to come. Curiously, the latter is listed twice in the current catalogue with two different product numbers. The 1/35 scale Sdkfz 234/2 released by Russian company Modelist in 2019 is a reboxed version of the Italeri kit.

At right: The box art for Italeri's Sdkfz 234/1 model in 1/35 scale. Based on the Puma kit which was originally released in 1980, this model was updated with new parts in 1996 and the latest version is a re-boxing. Despite its age this can produce an accurate and reasonably detailed replica. Below: The 1/56 scale Sdkfz 234/2 built and painted following the instructions. Of the major manufacturers, only Italeri produces models in this scale which is compatible with 28mm wargames figures.

EDUARD MODEL ACCESSORIES

Founded in 1989, this Czech company produces high quality photo-etched brass detail sets and a number of scale models. Upgrade sets are offered in 1/35 for all four armoured cars in the Sdkfz 234 series, which include interior details, and in 1/72 scale for the Sdkfz 234/2, specifically recommended for the Hasegawa kit. Although many of these items are marked as discontinued in the company's catalogue they are re-released from time to time and can be obtained from retailers.

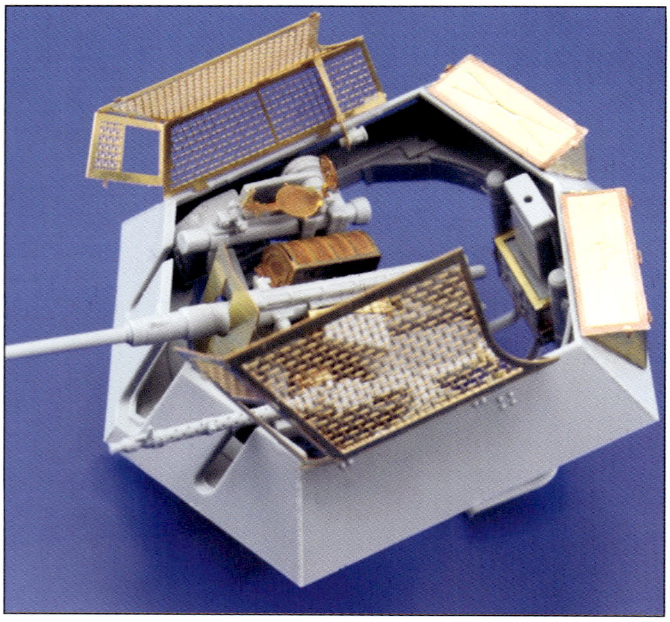

Above: The photo-etched brass details for the Sdkfz 234/1 turret in 1/35 scale including the protective mesh screen, ammunition containers and fittings, including the sights and gun shield, for the MG 34 machine gun and 2cm KwK 38 gun.

GRIFFON MODEL

This Chinese company was founded by a group of like-minded modelling enthusiasts and produces a large range of photo-etched brass sets for the Sdkfz 234 series armoured cars in 1/35 scale. While these will fit most manufacturers' models, the company does recommend Tamiya and Dragon.

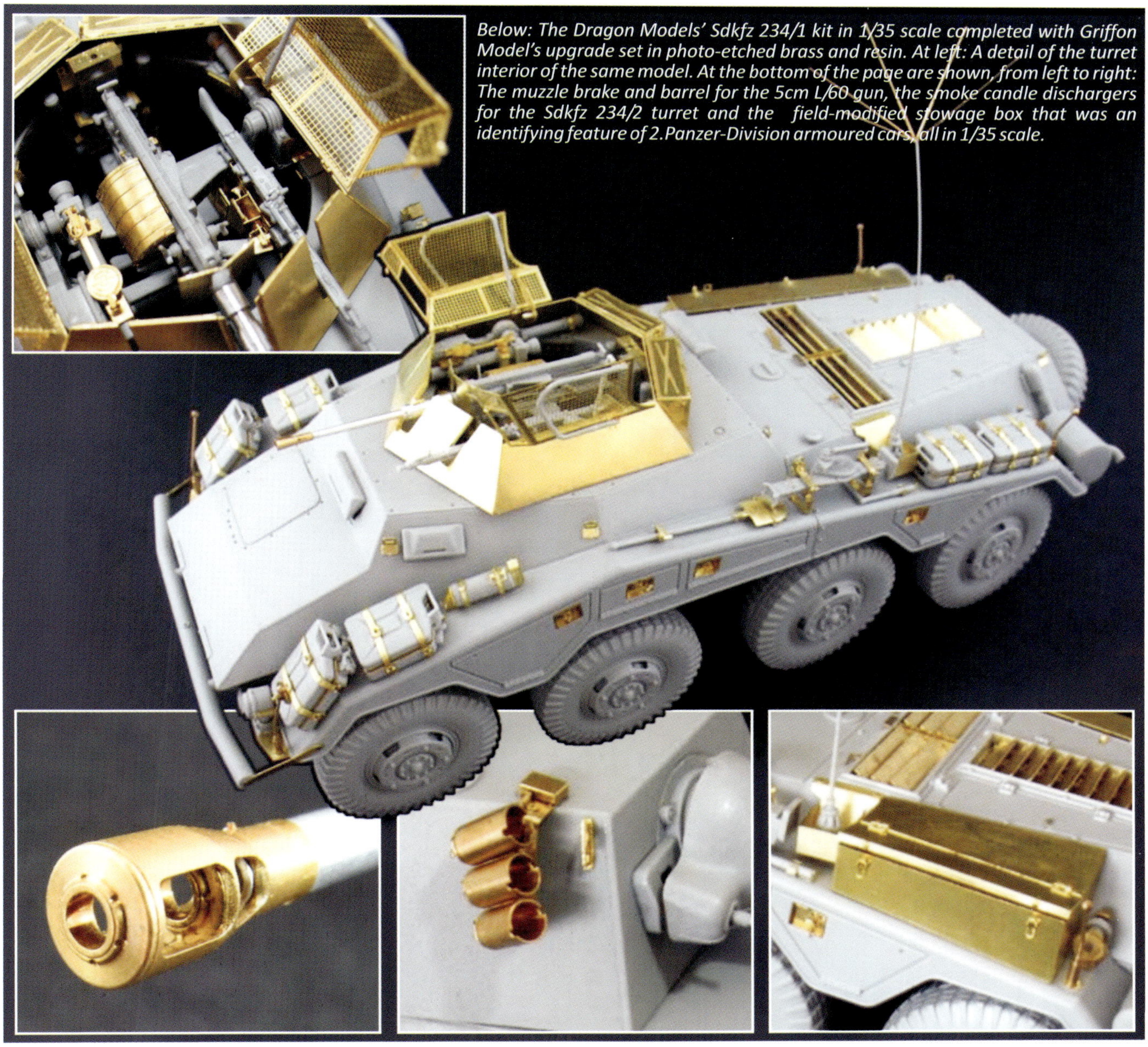

Below: The Dragon Models' Sdkfz 234/1 kit in 1/35 scale completed with Griffon Model's upgrade set in photo-etched brass and resin. At left: A detail of the turret interior of the same model. At the bottom of the page are shown, from left to right: The muzzle brake and barrel for the 5cm L/60 gun, the smoke candle dischargers for the Sdkfz 234/2 turret and the field-modified stowage box that was an identifying feature of 2.Panzer-Division armoured cars, all in 1/35 scale.

ROYAL MODEL

This Italian company has been producing high quality aftermarket parts since the early 1990s under the guidance of its founder, Roberto Reale. The current catalogue includes detailed upgrade sets in 1/35 scale for the Sdkfz 234/1 (shown below), Sdkfz 234/2 and Sdkfz 234/4. Materials used are photo-etched brass, aluminium and resin. The company markets these sets as appropriate for the Dragon Models' kits but they could also be use with Tamiya and Italeri 1/35 scale models.

VOYAGER MODEL

Voyager Model, based in Shanghai, have been manufacturing upgrade sets for scale models since 2003 with the release of their first set for 1/35 scale armour. The company has been featured in a number of the books in the TankCraft series and their range of accessories for the Sdkfz 234 armoured car series (shown below) is perhaps the largest and most comprehensive available. Admittedly these items do require a certain level of skill and experience but they add an extra dimension to the basic kit in many cases and some are quite affordable. The sets are marketed as being made for the kits of specific manufacturers but they would be suitable for most 1/35 scale replicas.

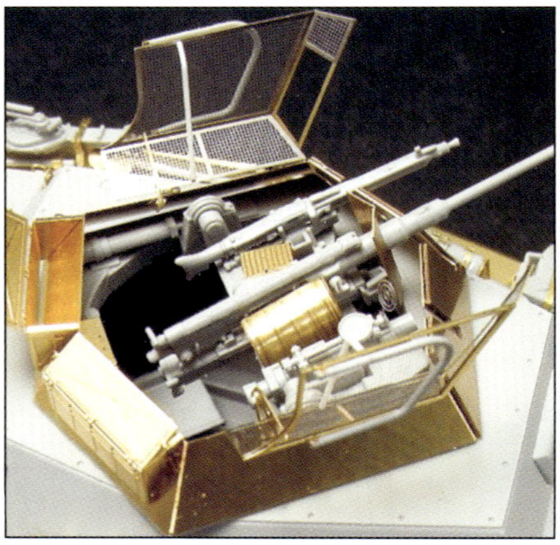

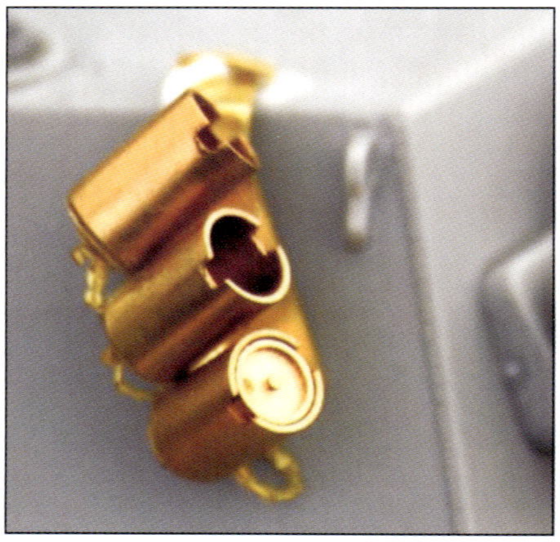

HAULER

Based in the Czech Republic, this company produces accessory sets in a variety of materials. At the time of writing the company's catalogue offered photo-etched brass upgrade sets for the Sdkfz 234/2 armoured car in 1/35 and 1/48 scale. While the parts are marketed as suitable for the Italeri kits they could be applied to the Tamiya and Dragon models. Similarly, many of the parts could also be used for the other vehicles of the Sdkfz 234 series, for example the engine air intake grills and the tools and brackets. The company also offers replacement wheels suitable for all the Sdkfz 234 series vehicles in 1/48 scale.

Far right: Photo-etched brass engine grills and replacement wheels in resin, both in in 1/35 scale, suitable for all Sdkfz 234 series armoured cars.

Above: Italeri's 1/35 scale Sdkfz 234/2 built with the Hauler upgrade set.

In the first part of this series, *LandCraft 11: Pakwagen Sdkfz 234/3 and 234/4 Heavy Armoured Cars, German Army, Waffen-SS and Luftwaffe Units, Western and Eastern Fronts, 1944–1945,* we examined the eight-wheeled vehicles manufactured by Büssing-NAG and armed with the 7.5cm L/24 gun and, its eventual replacement, the long-barrelled 7.5cm L/46 weapon. The latter was a slightly modified version of the army's towed anti-tank gun and will be familiar to many readers as the Pak 40. Although the Sdkfz 234 programme had been concerned from its inception with supplying the Aufklärungs battalions with a fighting edge that had been lacking with the earlier four- and six-wheeled designs, the new vehicles were increasingly used in close-support and tank-killing roles and in this section we will consider the technical aspects of the Sdkfz 234/1 and 234/2 which could fairly be said to have conformed to the army's doctrine of aggressive reconnaissance. These two models also represented the overwhelming bulk of production. To create a clear picture it is essential that some information from the first book is repeated here and I trust readers will forgive this.

Development of the Sdkfz 234 series of armoured cars had commenced in August 1940 when a specification for a replacement for the Sdkfz 231, which had been in service since 1937, was issued by Inspektorat (In) 6 of the Heereswaffenamt (1).

The project was initially referred to as Panzerspähwagen für Kolonialzwecke, or armoured car for use in undeveloped areas, and was based on the same 8-Rad, or eight-wheel, configuration as the Sdkfz 231 and also fitted with the 2cm KwK 38 gun. As originally envisaged the new design was similar in profile to its predecessor but the superstructure was to be strengthened with thicker armour and the armoured hull would itself serve as the chassis, unlike that of the earlier model which was built on a frame. The firm of Büssing-NAG, which had built the Sdkfz 231 and Sdkfz 232, was selected to manufacture the production version of the chassis and superstructure but the new armoured car was to be powered by an air-cooled diesel engine and a 12-cylinder model produced by Tatra-Werke AG, a company that had been producing automobile engines since 1895, was chosen.

By July 1941 the project had been renamed Actradwagen, abbreviated to ARK, and a report from that time confirms that the production design would be armed with the Rheinmetall 2cm KwK 38 fitted with the Flak-rohr barrel extention and that two development vehicles would be completed by Büssing-NAG and ready for testing by the following December.

.........................*text continued on page 51*

Notes

1. Put simply the Heereswaffenamt was the army's ordnance office. It oversaw the development and testing of new equipment in addition to the acceptance of weapons and vehicles and at one time was made up of approximately 7,000 military and civilian personnel. Inspektorat (In) 6 was responsible for armoured troops.

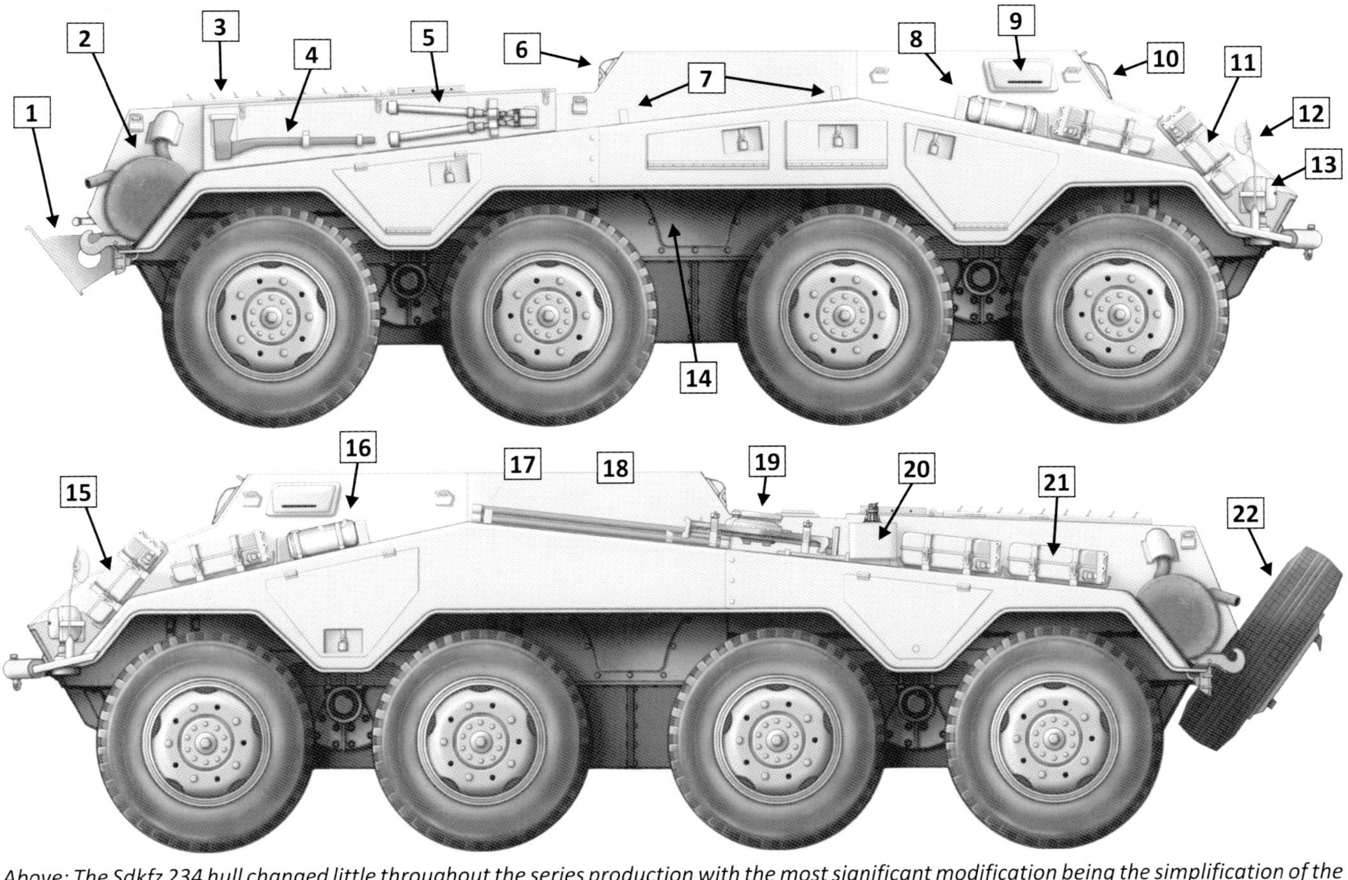

Above: The Sdkfz 234 hull changed little throughout the series production with the most significant modification being the simplification of the mudguards where the four-locker door version was replaced by a model with two doors on each side. The latter variant was probably introduced into production in December 1944. 1. Spare tyre bracket. 2. Exhaust muffler. 3. Engine deck ventilation grill. 4. Axe. 5. Wire cutters. 6. Driver's rear visor. 7. Brackets for long-handled shovel, right side. 8. Fire extinguisher, right side. 9. Driver's side visor. 10. Driver's front visor. 11. Fuel containers. 12. Rear vision mirror and width indicator, right side. 13. Bosch headlight, right side. 14. Hull ventilation hatch. 15. Fuel containers, left side. 16. Fire extinguisher, left side. 17. Bracket for long-handled shovel, left side. 18. Gun cleaning rods. 19. Jack. 20. Armoured cover for radio antenna insulator. 21. Fuel containers. 22. Spare tyre.

The interior of the Hängelafette 38 turret as depicted in an Allied intelligence publication. Although somewhat unclear, and lacking in descriptive detail, these pages are worth reproducing as there is no surviving example of an Sdkfz 234/1 armoured car. Note that I have enhanced some parts of these pages but retained the terms used in the originals. In photograph 1, at left: A. Frame. B. Fastener for ammunition box. C. Protective screen. D. Firing mechanism. E. Latch. F. Ammunition belt guide. G. Machine-gun firing cable. H. Left support. I. Middle support. J. Flange. K. Spent casing deflector. L. Right support. M. Right support arm. N. Geared segment. In photograph 2, right: A. 30mm thick armour. B. Cable pull 2cm KwK 38. C. Geared turret ring. D. Handwheel. E. Handle. F. Right cover plate. G. Roller guide. H. Firing lever 2cm KwK 38. I. Elevation lock. J. Firing lever MG 42. K. Positioning clamp. L. Left cover plate. M. Seat support tube. N. Adjusting bolt. O. Adjusting clamp. P. Seat. Q. Adjusting clamp. Below: A much clearer view of the Hängelafette 38 turret, here fitted to the Aufklärungspanzer 38. This is identical to the version fitted to the Sdkfz 234/1 and not mentioned in the pages above are: 1. The TZF 3a gun sight. Note the anti-aircraft ring, on the forward edge, in the lowered position. 2. FuG 5 radio antenna insulator. 3. Ammunition stowage locker.

........................text continued from page 49

This was probably the first time that the term Panzerspähwagen (Tp) 8-Radwagen was used, the Tp designation indicating Tropen or tropical.

At the same time Inspektorat 6 requested that development begin on a four-wheeled armoured car, referred to as the 4-Rad (Tp), which was basically a shortened version of the Actradwagen and this vehicle would also be armed with the 2cm KwK 38 mounted in a Hängelafette, or hanging mount, turret. Design work on the turret is reported to have begun as early as April 1940, suggesting that it predated the ARK programme, and although the four-wheeled project was eventually abandoned in late 1943, the Hängelafette turret was incorporated into Sdkfz 234 production.

Progress on the eight-wheeled design was slow and a report of 1 July 1942 stated that while the chassis design was considered ready to enter production, further trials were required of the diesel engine and these were expected to take place in Libya.

This is also the first time that the possiblity of fitting the new design with a modified 5cm KwK 39 gun is mentioned and Daimler-Benz was tasked with producing a suitable turret for this weapon. Despite the inevitable delays that this decision was sure to entail, Büssing-NAG was awarded a contract for 500 vehicles with the first production models to be ready within exactly twelve months. Production of the 5cm-armed vehicle was to take place alongside the version fitted with the Hängelafette turret but manufacturing delays and indecision regarding the production ratios meant that the first models were not completed until December 1943. Initially referred to as schwere Panzerspähwagen (5cm 39/1 L/60) (Sdkfz 234), the official designation of these first vehicles was not changed to Sdkfz 234/2 until March 1944.

The first examples of the 2cm-armed version did not leave the assembly lines until the following June, by which time it was referred to as the Sdkfz 234/1. Both variants utilised the same hull and suspension and we should examine the major difference, the turrets, before considering the technical details of the Sdkfz 234 chassis.

The Sdkfz 234/1 turret. As with most aspects of the Sdkfz 234 programme there are seemingly contradictory reports regarding the development of the Hängelafette 38 turret. The July 1941 specification for the 4-Rad (Tp) armoured

Above: Examples of the armoured car turrets, leading to the development of the Hängelafette 38, mentioned in the text. 1. The welded turret of the Sdkfz 232 eight-wheeled armoured car of the so-called fourth or fifth series production. At least one of the Sdkfz 234 prototypes was fitted with this turret although photographs would suggest that the 2cm KwK 38 was missing. 2. The open-topped turret originally designed for the Sdkfz 222 armoured car and later fitted to the early version of the Sdkfz 250 halftrack as shown here. The wire mesh screen has been removed. 3. The production version of the Hängelafette 38, here fitted to an Aufklärungspanzer 38(t). This is identical to the Sdkfz 234/1 version. 4. The Hängelafette 38 fitted to an Sdkfz 234/2. This interesting view also shows the driver's rear visor and the shape of the hull stowage box.

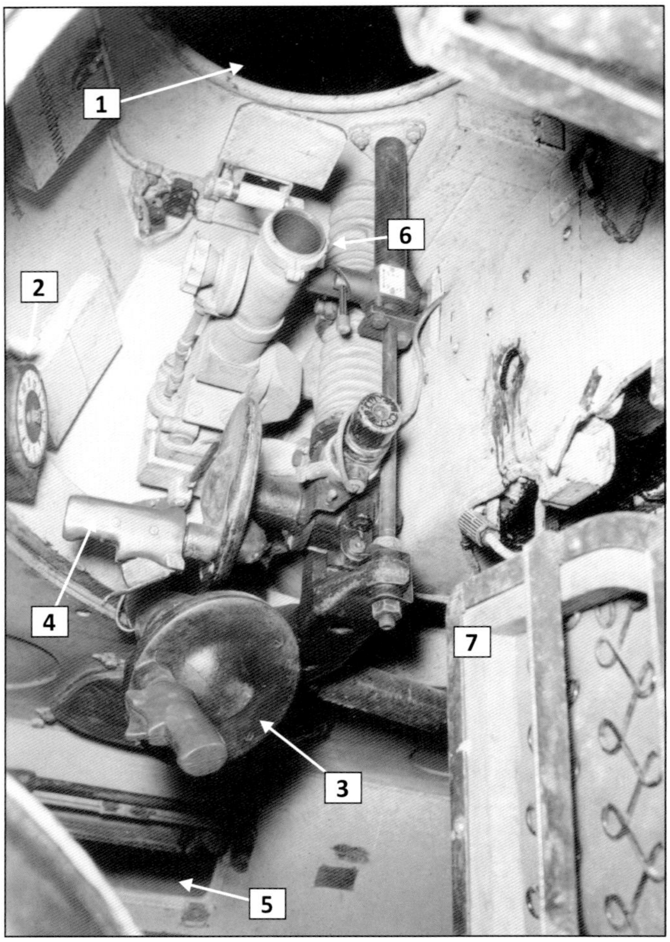

Above: The interior of the Daimler-Benz turret looking forward. Points to note are: 1. The open gunner's hatch. 2. The azimuth indicator on the turret ring. 3. The traversing handwheel, incorporating an electrical firing mechanism, turned with the gunner's right hand. 4. The elevation handwheel, turned with the gunner's left hand. 5. Driver's forward visor. 6. The T.Z.F. 4b telescopic sight. Note that the eye piece has been lost. 7. The gunner's seat, turned to the right. 8. The auxiliary hand traverse next to the commander's position. 9. Ammunition bags for the machine gun spent casings. 10. The T.Rb1.F.3 binocular observation periscope. 11. The parts box (Ergängkasten) for the periscope, as noted on the interior wall (12). 13. Machine gun cleaning kit.

car mentions that design work on the turret had begun as early as April 1940 by Gustav Appel Maschinenfabrik at the company's Berlin-Spandau factory. But this firm was better known for the manufacture of tools and small pieces of equipment, most famously gun cleaning kits. A report of 1 July 1942 states that the turret was designed and manufactured by the firm of F. Schichau at Elbing, modern-day Elblag in Poland, and this is almost certainly correct (1).

The turret was six-sided and featured an open top protected by a mesh screen which could be opened outwards. The armour thickness varied between 30mm at the front, with an additional 10mm for the gun shield, and 8mm on the sides and rear. It was traversable, by hand, through 360 degrees. Although the design was obviously influenced by the Sockellafette turret of the Sdkfz 222 light armoured car, it was not supported by a pedestal, as the earlier version was, and seats for the gunner and commander, who also acted as the loader, were suspended in the turret ring. Although it was of approximately the same width as the Sockellafette turret the Hängelafette 38 was considerably longer and offered more room for the crew. A TZF 3a sight was used to engage ground targets but the 2cm gun was also considered an effective weapon against enemy aircraft. Stowage was provided for 250 rounds of 2cm ammunition and 2,400 rounds for the MG 42.

Although it was anticipated that the first 2cm-armed vehicles would leave the assembly plants in July 1943 it was not until June 1944 that the first armoured cars, now designated Sdkfz 234/1, were delivered. Production continued until the end of the war and in addition to the 200 examples of the Sdkfz 234/1 assembled by Büssing-NAG, the Hängelafette 38 was fitted to the Aufklärungspanzer 38 and the later version of the Sdkfz 250/9 halftrack (2).

The Sdkfz 234/2 turret. As mentioned earlier the initial specification for the 8-Rad (Tp) armoured car had envisaged that a version of the 2cm KwK 38 would be the main armament but by July 1942 a report was submitted that stated that a detailed design for a turret fitted with the 5cm KwK 39 was being undertaken by Daimler-Benz (3).

.........................*text continued on page 54*

Notes

1. A photograph of one of the trial chassis taken at this time shows it fitted with the turret of an Sdkfz 232 armoured car which would suggest that a final version of the Hängelafette 38 was still some way off.
2. The production of the earlier version of this vehicle, with a modified Sdkfz 222 turret, may be where the suggestion of the involvement of Gustav Appel Maschinenfabrik in the Hängelafette 38 design originated.
3. Although a report of the same date credits F. Schichau with involvement in the development of the new turret this is more indicative of the confusion generated by the resultant changes in production ratios.

An Sdkfz 234/2 of 1.Kompanie, Panzer-Aufklärungs-Abteilung 2 photographed after the Normandy battles. Note the metal racks for the fuel containers on the front mudguards and the remains of the canvas straps. Note also the ammunition box welded to the mudguard and the large field-modified stowage box behind the radio antenna which was an identifying feature of this battalion. This vehicle is also shown in the Camouflage & Markings section on page 18.

The Daimler-Benz production turret for the Sdkfz 234/2 armoured car. Points to note are: 1. Smoke candle dischargers. 2. Turret lifting hook. 3. MG 42 aperture. 4. Topfblende main gun mantlet. 5. T.Rb1.F.3 observation periscope in raised position. 6. Radio antenna insulator. 7. Commander's hatch with armoured periscope cover. 8. Gunner's hatch with armoured periscope cover. 9. Aperture for T.Z.F. 4b Leitz gun sight.

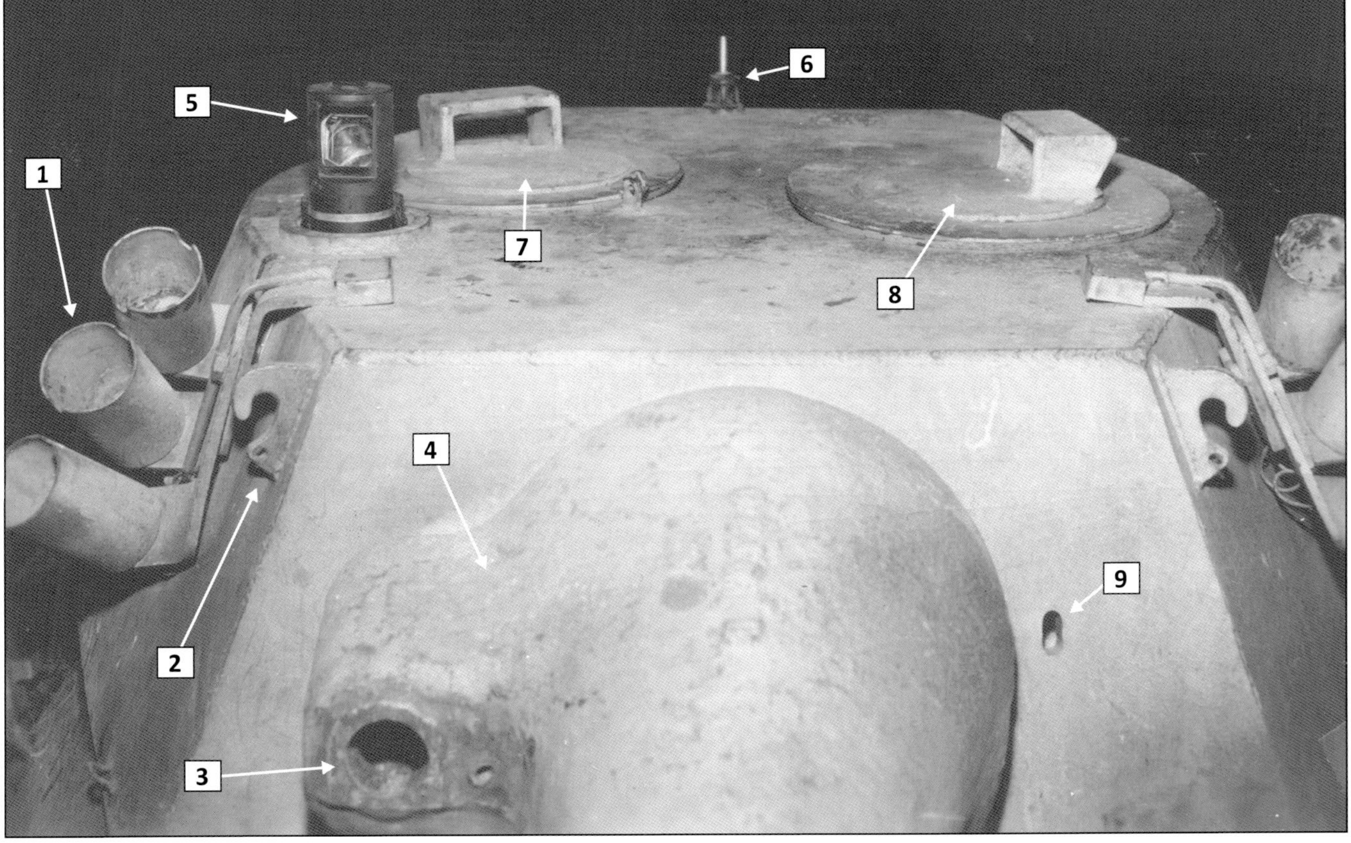

........................text continued from page 49

The turret was also intended to be used in the Luchs and Leopard programmes which were also in the development stage at that time (1).

The Daimler-Benz turret was to be fully enclosed and in addition to the main gun was armed with a coaxial MG 42. It was to be fabricated of welded armour plate of 30mm thickness for the front, 14.5mm for the sides and 10mm for the turret roof. The gunner sat on the left side while the commander, who also acted as the loader, sat on the right. Large hatch covers were provided for each and both covers were fitted with Winkelspiegel R periscopes which were traversable through 360 degrees.

Installed in the turret roof, in front of the commander, was a T.Rb1.F.3 observation periscope which could be raised or lowered. The use of this periscope required that the vehicle remain stationary. The turret could be traversed manually by a hand wheel, which also incorporated an electrical firing mechanism, through 360 degrees and this required 180 turns. The main armament was to be the 5cm KwK 39/1, a development of the 5cm L/60 weapon fitted to the later models of the Pzkpfw III which Rheinmetall had reworked to fit the narrow Daimler Benz turret.

The gun was mounted in a cast mantlet, referred to as a Topfblende, and this also held the coaxial machine gun. The difficulty of obtaining parts for the Topfblende would lead to delays in delivery of the 5cm-armed vehicle and the plan to complete the first vehicles by July 1943 was not realised until the following December. Stowage was provided for fifty-five rounds of 5cm ammunition, typically twenty-seven Panzergranate 39 and twenty-eight Sprenggranate 38, armour-piercing and high-explosive ordnance respectively.

The designation Sdkfz 234/2 was not introduced until March 1944 and production ended in the following June after approximately 100 vehicles had been assembled.

Notes

1. The turret of the Pzkpfw II ausf L Luchs was completely redesigned and the Leopard project was abandoned before the first prototype was completed.

Final assembly of the Sdkfz 234 series of armoured cars took place at the Büssing-NAG plant in Braunschweig and several types of wheel and wheel hub arrangement were fitted during the course of production. The different wheel hubs can be divided into two broad categories: those with two cut-outs on the outer edge next to the rim, and those with five. The cut-outs on both types could be rounded or more squared-off and the latter seem to have predominated as production went on. All were held in place by five bolts with an extra hole drilled between each and this may have been to facilitate their use with the company's heavy lorries, particularly the Type 4500 S and T series, which had very similar wheels and hubs and required ten bolts. It should be remembered that many smaller companies were involved in component manufacture and this would explain some minor differences. Shown above are examples of the wheel hubs. 1. An Sdkfz 234/3 captured intact in France during the late summer or early autumn of 1944. This very rounded version, with almost circular cut-outs, may have been fitted to the first production vehicles of this model. 2. An Sdkfz 234/2 of Panzer-Lehr-Division photographed in Normandy. This vehicle must have been assembled before March 1944 and the hub is slightly more raised than later versions. 3. An Sdkfz 234/1 assembled at some time after December 1944 fitted with what seems to have been the most commonly-used wheel hub. It is noticeably flatter that the version shown in 2 and the cut-outs are quite angular. 4. An Sdkfz 234/3 photographed in April 1945. The wheel hub has a rounded outer edge with rounded cut-outs. Production features on this vehicle suggest that it was assembled during December 1944, perhaps one of the last production models. 5. An Sdkfz 234/4 photographed in Germany in April 1945. This is another view of the wheel hub shown in 4. 6. The wheel hub of an Sdkfz 234/4 abandoned in northern Germany in May 1945. Note the very angular edge of the wheel hub and the two cut-outs. I have been able to identify at least eight different tyre patterns from photographs and three are visible here.

An aspect of the manufacturing process which affected all armoured vehicles was the application of camouflage paint, either as a base colour or as a disruptive pattern. This subject was covered in detail in the first part of this series and I will restrict this section to a brief discussion of the history of the camouflage colours involved and show how this relates to the Sdkfz 234/1 and Sdkfz 234/2 armoured cars. But as production of the different models of the Sdkfz 234 series overlapped, and was undertaken at the same factory, some mention of the 7.5cm-armed versions is essential to enable a full understanding. I should also acknowledge that very little official documentation regarding the standardised camouflage schemes applied to German armoured vehicles has survived the war and most of the findings I have presented here are based on contemporary photographs, allocation lists and unit histories (1).

Most readers will be familiar with the three-colour camouflage introduced in February 1943 that replaced the overall covering of Schwartzgrau RAL 7021, a very dark grey shade. In general, vehicles now left the assembly plants in a colour at first referred to as Dunkelgelb nach Muster and later as Dunkelgelb RAL 7028, a dark yellow with a hint of green. Formations were to be provided with two camouflage colours, initially RLM Olivgrün and Rotbraun RAL 8017.

The intention was that units in the field, taking into consideration the conditions of the local terrain and climate, could best devise an effective camouflage scheme for their armoured vehicles. Importantly, this also saw the end to the practice of formations sourcing paint directly from commercial suppliers and a subsequent directive issued in April 1943 contained a table indicating the exact amount of paint required, by weight, to cover a specific type of vehicle (2).

As production of the Sdkfz 234/2 ran from December 1943 to June 1944 all these vehicles would have been finished in a coat of Dunkelgelb (3).

Both the Sdkfz 234/1 and Sdkfz 234/3 versions began series production in June 1944 with the last vehicles leaving the assembly lines in March 1945 and December 1944 respectively. Manufacture of the Sdkfz 234/3 ended abruptly and it was replaced on the assmbly lines by the Sdkfz 234/4, production of which finished in April 1945, just weeks before the end of the war. These date are significant as they dictate the application of camouflage paint as we shall see.

The importance of the economic use of paint had been mentioned in every major order regarding vehicle camouflage issued since the beginning of the war and over time it must have became clear that the system introduced in February 1943, although flexible, was prone to waste and on 19 August 1944 the Heereswaffenamt advised the assembly plants that the practice of units in the field creating their own patterns of camouflage would halt immediately. Henceforth, a standard scheme would be applied to vehicles before they left the factories. The base colour of Dunkelgelb was to be retained, over which

Notes

1. The colours mentioned here were part of the coding system instituted by the Reichs-Ausschuss für Lieferbedingungen und Gütesicherung (RAL) in 1927 and revised in 1941 as the Farbtonregister 840-R.
2. The April directive also replaced RLM Olivgrün, a Luftwaffe colour, with Olivgrün RAL 6003. It was also the first occasion when Dunkelgelb was referred to as RAL 7028.
3. It is true that allocations were made as late as January 1945 but these were vehicles which had been held at the arsenals since at least September 1944 or returned from repair in the following October.

Photographed near Pilsen, modern-day Plzen in the Czech Republic, this Sdkfz 234/2 of Stabskompanie, Panzer-Aufklärungs-Abteilung 20 provides a good comparison between the camouflage patterns created by units in the field using Rotbraun and Olivgrün on a Dunkelgelb base coat and the hard-edged factory-applied scheme visible on the Jagdpanzer 38 in the background at right. This armoured car is also shown and discussion on page 25 of the Camouflage & Markings section of this book.

At left: Photographed in Germany towards the end of the war, this Sdkfz 234/1 has traces of a factory-applied camouflage scheme visible on the hull front and the open hull access door. The cover on the turret is not the standard-issue item, as fitted to the armoured car shown below, but seems to be made up from several Zeltbahn tent quarters. The boxes fixed to the later-style front mudguard between the fire extinguisher and fuel container were a common modification seen on vehicles of Panzer-Aufklärungs-Abteilung 20 but any definitive identification is not possible.

At right: While this image is of mediocre quality it is very interesting as it presents a rare top view of the factory-applied camouflage which appears to be the pattern referred to here as Type II. Note that the contours visible on the hull front, particularly across the access door, correspond to those applied to the vehicles shown above but are slightly different around the driver's visor. The canvas turret cover, which is also camouflaged, was also produced for the Sdkfz 234/4 at this time. Note also the non-standard stowage box on the right side mudguard.

large patches of Olivgrün and Rotbraun were to be painted. Templates which showed how these colours were to be applied accompanied the orders and it was stressed that although every effort was to be made to deliver the remaining August consignment in the new factory-applied schemes, production was not to be impeded due to a lack of the appropriate camouflage colours.

In late October 1944 a directive issued by the Heereswaffenamt stipulated that component manufacturers and assembly plants were to cease the use of Dunkelgelb RAL 7028 as a base colour for the exterior surfaces of armoured vehicles. Over the basic primer colour a camouflage scheme made up of what was described as patches of Rotbraun, Olivgrün and Dunkelgelb was to be applied once the assembly process had been finalised (1).

In spite of the directives there is ample evidence that many manufacturers did not begin painting their vehicles in the new schemes in August or even October 1944 and continued to use Dunkelgelb as the base coat for some time.

In any case, by 29 November 1944, the Heereswaffenamt had advised vehicle manufacturers that a new system was to be introduced where the armour components were to be painted in a base coat of Dunkelgrün RAL 6003, referred to in previous orders as Olivgrün, before they were delivered to the assembly plants. Once the tank was ready for shipment it was to be camouflaged by the addition of patches of Rotbraun and Dunkelgelb painted in sharp contours. The actual implementation of this scheme was not to take place until 1 March 1945 but a new order, dated 20 December, directed that the painting of armour components in Dunkelgrün was to begin immediately. Just five days later, on Christmas Day 1944, a memorandum titled Anstrich des Heeresgerät was disseminated and this went into more detail regarding how different surfaces were to be coated. I would suggest that at about this time Sdkfz 234/4 and Sdkfz 234/1 production vehicles began leaving the Büssing-NAG plant painted in the three-colour camouflage scheme referred to here as Type I (2).

It was at some time in December 1944 that production of the Sdkfz 234/3 was switched to the Sdkfz 234/4 and at least two photographs exist of the new models finished in a coat of plain Dunkelgelb, suggesting that the factory-applied schemes were not introduced at Büssing-NAG until the year was almost over. One image shows an 234/4 vehicle fitted with the early pattern mudguards confirming that it was one of the first production models (3).

Notes

1. This is referred to in some documents as the Sparanstrich, or economy coating. Many accounts assume that the primer formed part of the camouflage scheme but it is clear that the October directive was merely intended to reduce the amount of Dunkelgelb paint.
2. I should stress that the terms Type I and Type II are my invention and created for this series to explain an apparent difference in the sytyle of factory-applied camouflage employed by Büssing-NAG.
3. This photograph is reproduced in *LandCraft 11: Pakwagen Sdkfz 234/3 and 234/4 Heavy Armoured Cars, German Army, Waffen-SS and Luftwaffe Units, Western and Eastern Fronts, 1944–1945.*

Of all the many photographs I have been able to examine I have been unable to find a single example of an Sdkfz 234/3 armoured car finished in one of the factory-applied schemes. Indeed, a photograph taken in May 1945 shows an Sdkfz 234/3 armoured car fitted with the later-pattern mudguards, which would suggest that it was one of the last production models built in November or December 1944, and painted in a very light colour, almost certainly Dunkelgelb, without any additional camouflage.

Confirming the December directive, Heeres-Verordnungsblatt Nr.52 dated 3 February 1945 (1) stated that vehicles were to receive a base coat of Dunkelgrün RAL 6003 which was to be camouflaged with Rotbraun and Dunkelgelb applied in equal amounts, with the green shade as the predominant colour. The camouflage was to be completed after final assembly and a template or guide was provided. It is possible that the factory-applied scheme referred to here as Type II was introduced as a result of this directive.

Although exact production figures are not available, it is known that eleven Sdkfz 234/1 armoured cars were delivered to the Heereswaffenamt in December 1944. The thirty-seven vehicles accepted in the following month are the last about which we have precise information and these may account for the allocations made in January and February 1945.

A further twenty-one Sdkfz 234/1 armoured cars were assigned to units before the end of the war and it is possible that these were painted in the Type II scheme although we can only speculate at this stage.

Notes

1. Heeres-Verordnungsblatt were orders dealing with unclassified information and this instruction, as detailed as it is, may have been intended to clarify the current position for the manufacturers concerned. This document is the earliest I have been able to locate which specifically mentions Dunkelgelb RAL 7028 Ausgabe 1944, a slightly darker version of the colour introduced in February 1943.

At left: An Sdkfz 234/1 armoured car photographed in early 1945 and painted in one of the the factory-applied camouflage schemes. Note the later-pattern mudguard with two locker doors which was probably introduced into production in December 1944. Although it is not possible to identify colour with any certainty from a monochrome image, it appears that the wheel hubs have also been painted in the three standard camouflage colours of Rotbraun, Olivgrün and Dunkelgelb. Below: The factory-applied scheme that I have classified here as Type I. Note that the darkest shade, Rotbraun (A). Note also the complicated shapes around the forward hull and mudguard.

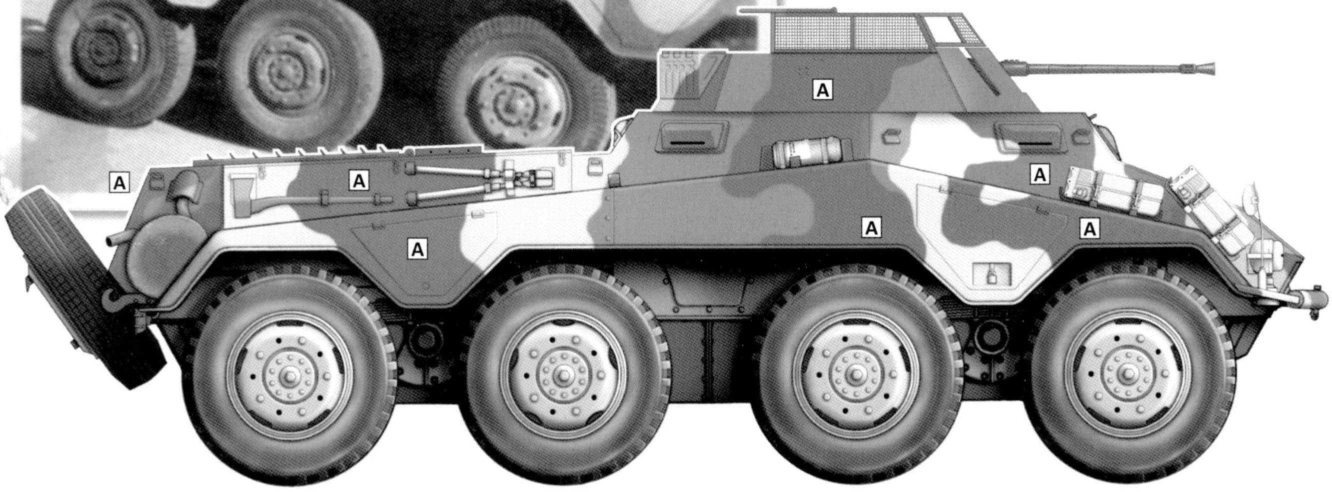

Below: The Type II camouflage scheme. The proportion of Olivgrün (B) has increased slightly but the most significant feature is the simplification of some of the more complicated shapes. This scheme may have been introduced in February or very early March 1945 and it is the most commonly seen in period photographs, particularly those depicting Sdkfz 234/4 vehicles. The wheels appear, in most cases, to have been painted but as many of the available photographs show damaged or worn vehicles it is difficult to be certain. Photographs suggest that the pattern applied to the left side remained unchanged from the Type I.

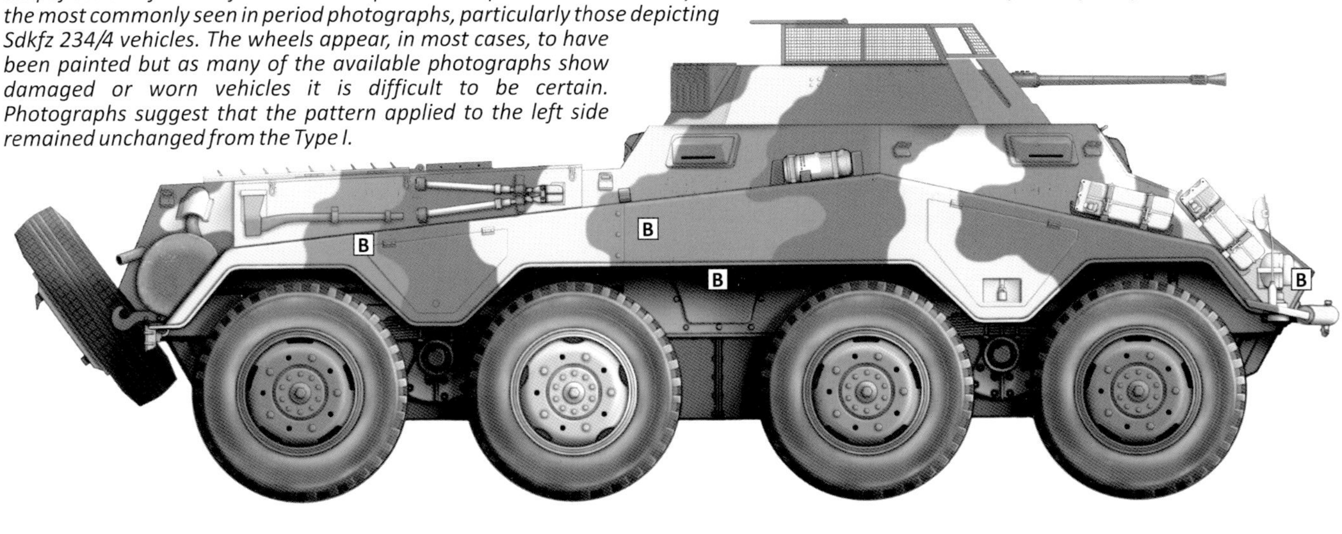

SDKFZ 234 ALLOCATIONS, 1943-1945

The figures given here were obtained for the most part from the Zuführungliste, or shipping lists, compiled by the Heereswaffenamt between May 1943 and April 1945. Unfortunately vehicles are often referred to simply as Panzerspähwagen, although some monthly totals are broken up into heavy or light, but usually without mention of a specific type. Therefore some information is based on other sources, for example Kriegsgliederungen, or unit organisations, and production figures where they exist. Readers will notice that the total number of vehicles shipped does not correspond to the number of armoured cars assembled.

Month	Vehicle Type				Unit
	Sdkfz 234/1	Sdkfz 234/2	Sdkfz 234/3	Sdkfz 234/4	
Total Production	200	101	88	88	

Production figures for these vehicles are possibly incomplete and those given here are based on the following: Sdkfz 234/1, 163 vehicles assembled in 1944 and 37 in 1945; Sdkfz 234/2, 7 vehicles assembled in 1943 and 94 in 1944; Sdkfz 234/3, 88 vehicles assembled in 1944 before production ceased abruptly in December; Sdkfz 234/4, 25 vehicles assembled in 1944 and 73 in 1945. Note that some sources give the total production figure for the latter of 89.

September 1943		1			Panzertruppen-Schule II (1)
October 1943		1			Panzertruppen-Schule II

1. Panzertruppen-Schule II, located at Krampnitz near Berlin, was the second of the army's two major armoured schools. In March 1944 it was renamed Panzertruppenschule Krampnitz. Panzertruppenschule I was based at Wünsdorf, just south of Zossen, until March 1944 when it was moved to Bergen and renamed Panzertruppenschule Bergen. Both establishments were amalgamated in October 1944.

November 1943					
December 1943		1			Aufklärungs-Lehr-Abteilung (2)

2. This unit was later renamed as Aufklärungs-Abteilung 130 and attached to Panzer-Lehr-Division.

January 1944		5			Aufklärungs-Lehr-Abteilung
February 1944		6			Aufklärungs-Lehr-Abteilung
		6			7.Panzer-Division
March 1944		14			Aufklärungs-Lehr-Abteilung
		4			2.Panzer-Division
April 1944		21			2.Panzer-Division
		2 (3)			Ersatzheer

3. A handwritten note on the allocation list for April 1944 states that these vehicles were eventually handed over from theErsatzheer to Aufklärungs-Lehr-Abteilung and 2.Panzer-Division.

May 1944		16			1.SS-Panzer-Division
		1			Ersatzheer
June 1944		16			20.Panzer-Division
		1			Ersatzheer
		1			SS-Ersatzheer
July 1944			3		9.Panzer-Division
			3		11.Panzer-Division
		1 (4)			Ersatzheer
			3		6.Panzer-Division
			1 (5)		Panzer-Aufklärungs-Lehr-Kompanie Krampnitz
	16				9.Panzer-Division
	13	1 (6)	3		116.Panzer-Division
	16				11.Panzer-Division

4. This vehicle may have later been allocated to 4.Kompanie, Panzer-Aufklärungs-Lehr-Abteilung Krampnitz.
5. The vehicle type is uncertain and the allocation is based on the shipping lists for that month.
6. Originally allocated to the Ersatzheer.

August 1944	3				6.Panzer-Division
	4		3		2.SS-Panzer-Division
			3		8.Panzer-Division
September 1944	9				2.SS-Panzer-Division
	13				8.Panzer-Division
	10				6.Panzer-Division
	6				Führer-Grenadier-Brigade
	3				20.Panzer-Division
		1			Ersatzheer
October 1944	3		5		1.SS-Panzer-Division
	8				Panzer-Lehr-Division
	13		3		Fallschirm-Panzer-Division Hermann Göring
	1		3		12.SS-Panzer-Division
	4		2		20.Panzergrenadier-Division
		2	3		Ersatzheer
November 1944	2				Panzer-Lehr-Division
	2	2 (7)			2.Panzer-Division
	4		3		9.SS-Panzer-Division
	10 (8)		2		9.Panzer-Division
	4		1		116.Panzer-Division
	3				12.SS-Panzer-Division
		3	3		Panzer-Brigade 150
			3		Panzergrenadier-Division Brandenburg

7. Provisional, perhaps repaired and returned.
8. The ten Sdkfz 234/1 vehicles were actually delivered to 9.SS-Panzer-Division in error.

Month	Vehicle Type				Unit
	Sdkfz 234/1	Sdkfz 234/2	Sdkfz 234/3	Sdkfz 234/4	
Total Production	200	101	88	88	

Production figures for these vehicles are possibly incomplete and those given here are based on the following: Sdkfz 234/1, 163 vehicles assembled in 1944 and 37 in 1945; Sdkfz 234/2, 7 vehicles assembled in 1943 and 94 in 1944; Sdkfz 234/3, 88 vehicles assembled in 1944 before production ceased abruptly in December; Sdkfz 234/4, 25 vehicles assembled in 1944 and 73 in 1945. Note that some sources give the total production figure for the latter of 89.

December 1944	3		3		10.SS-Panzer-Division
	4				Panzergrenadier-Division Brandenburg
			3		4.SS-Polizei-Division
			3 (9)		Panzer-Aufklärungs-Lehr-Kompanie
			2		Ersatzheer
			1		Panzer-Division Feldherrnhalle
			1		1.Panzer-Division
			2		13.Panzer-Division
			1		23.Panzer-Division
			3		24.Panzer-Division
	8		1 (10)		1.Kompanie, Panzer-Aufklärungs-Abteilung 190
		3 (11)			7.Panzer-Division
			3		17.SS-Panzergrenadier-Division

9. Not to be confused with Panzer-Aufklärungs-Abteilung 130 of the Panzer-Lehr-Division. This unit later formed part of Radfahr-Jäger-Brigade 10 and these vehicles were probably still on hand when the brigade's I.Bataillon took part in the fighting around Elbing in January 1945 where several self-propelled 7.5cm guns are mentioned.
10. This unit became part of Panzer-Brigade 103 as Panzer-Aufklärungs-Abteilung Sternberg.
11. These Sdkfz 234/2 armoured cars may have been the last vehicles of this type to be issued to a front-line unit by the HZA. See note 12 below.

January 1945		2 (12)		7	Panzergrenadier-Division Brandenburg
				5	10.Panzergrenadier-Division
	3				Panzer-Aufklärungs-Lehr-Kompanie
			2		Panzer-Division Feldherrnhalle
	2		1		Panzer-Aufklärungs-Abteilung München
	8			7 (13)	24.Panzer-Division
	6	1			Ersatzheer
	1				Polizei-Schule Wien
	4				3.SS-Panzer-Division
	1		3		1.Kompanie, Panzer-Aufklärungs-Abteilung 190
	1			6 (14)	4.Panzer-Division

12. This number is provisional and is based on the total of nine vehicles shipped to the division. A notation on the Zuführungliste suggests that only seven were received. The two Sdkfz 234/2 are mentioned in a number of sources but their origins are unclear.
13. The division's Panzer-Aufklärungs-Abteilung 24 contained the army's only complete Type 45 Stabskompanie.
14. It is almost certain that the complete allocation of seven vehicles were in fact Sdkfz 234/1.

February 1945	4			6	Führer-Begleit-Division
	5			3	Panzergrenadier-Division Kurmark
	2		1		25.Panzergrenadier-Division
				3	Fallschirm-Panzer-Division Hermann Göring
				3 (15)	Panzer-Division Jüterbog
				3 (16)	Panzer-Division Schlesien

15. On 22 February 1945 Panzer-Division Jüterbog was absorbed by 16.Panzer-Division and the three Sdkfz 234/4 were handed over to Panzer-Aufklärungs-Abteilung 16.
16. Panzer-Division Schlesien was disbanded in mid-February 1945 and used to form Panzer-Division Holstein. These three vehicles were supposed to be handed over to the division's Panzer-Aufklärungs-Abteilung 44 but only one is reported as being on hand. The remnants of Panzer-Division Holstein were integrated into 18. Panzergrenadier-Division in March 1945.

March 1945	4			3	25.Panzer-Division
	4			4	Panzer-Division Müncheberg
	3			2	Panzerkorps-Feldherrnhalle
	4			3	13.Panzer-Division
				3	Fallschirm-Panzer-Division Hermann Göring
				4	8.Panzer-Division
	3			3	Begleitkompanie 1

With the exception of 25.Panzer-Division, Panzer-Division Müncheberg and Begleitkompanie 1 these numbers are all provisional.

April 1945				2	116.Panzer-Division
	3 (17)				Fallschirm-Panzer-Division Hermann Göring
				2 (18)	25.Panzergrenadier-Division
				2 (19)	Panzer-Aufklärungs-Abteilung Elbe/Döring

17. Provisional figure. 18. Provisional figure.
19. A notation on the Zuführungliste suggests that these may have been the two vehicles allocated to 116.Panzer-Division and shipped on 15 April 1945. Panzer-Aufklärungs-Abteilung Elbe/Döring was attached to Panzer-Division Clausewitz.

PANZER-AUFKLÄRUNGS-ABTEILUNG, LATE 1943

All formations of the German Army were organised according to detailed tables of establishment referred to as Kriegstärkenachweisung (KstN) which showed the official composition of a unit, listing the exact number of personnel and type of equipment from vehicles to small arms. The tables were numbered and dated, the latter being all-important as some numbers were often duplicated. The KstN were accompanied by Kriegsausrüstungsnachweisung (KAN) which listed minor items in detail such as tools and fuel containers but these need not concern us here. KstN 1162a dated 1 October 1943, a temporary order, was introduced to facilitate the introduction of the Sdkfz 234 series of armoured cars into service and this was formalised by KstN 1162a of 1 November 1943. This allowed for a single Sdkfz 234/2 at the company headquarters with a further six in each of the four platoons giving a total of twenty-five vehicles. It should be noted that only the reconnaissance battalions of 2.Panzer-Division and Panzer-Lehr-Division were fully equipped using this organisation and the Aufklärungs-Abteilungen of other Panzer formations were built using earlier establishments or KstN 1162d dated 1 March 1944.

Stab einer Panzer-Aufklärungsabteilung (gepanzert)
KstN 1109 (gp) von 1 November 1943

Versorgungs-Kompanie
einer Panzer-Aufklärungs-Abteilung (gepanzert)
KstN 1180 (gp) von 1 November 1943

Kfz-Instandsetzungs-Gruppe | Gefecktstross | Gepäcktstross

1.Kompanie as
Panzerspähwagen-Kompanie a
KstN 1162a von 1 November 1943

Gruppe Führer und Kompanietrupp

Sdkfz 234/2 *2 x Kettenkrad* *2 x Motorcycle* *Kfz 2 VW Car*

1.Zug
6 x Sdkfz 234/2

2.Zug *As for 1.Zug*

3.Zug *As for 1.Zug*

4.Zug *As for 1.Zug*

Alternate 1.Kompanie as
Panzerspähwagen-Kompanie d
KstN 1162d von 1 March 1944

Gruppe Führer und Kompanietrupp

Sdkfz 234/1 *2 x Kettenkrad* *2 x Motorcycle* *Kfz 2 VW Car*

1.Zug
2.Zug
und
3.Zug
Each with
6 x Sdkfz 234/2

4.(schwere)
Zug
6 x Sdkfz 234/3

2.Kompanie as
Panzerspähwagen-Kompanie c
KstN 1162c von 1 November 1943

9 x Sdkfz 250/5, 16 x Sdkfz 250/9

3.Kompanie as
Panzer-Aufklärungs-Kompanie (gepanzert)
KstN.1113 (gp) von 1 November 1943

4.Kompanie as
Panzer-Aufklärungs-Kompanie (gepanzert)
KstN.1113 (gp) von 1 November 1943

These companies were organised identically and at full strength contained 59 x Sdkfz 250/1, 2 x Sdkfz 250/3, 2 x Sdkfz 250/7 and 2 x Sdkfz 250/8. The inclusion of the latter was somewhat premature as these vehicles did not enter service until the summer of 1944.

5.(schwere) Kompanie

This support company was made up of Teileinheiten (TE), or parts, of a number of KstN as follows: (TE) Führer schwere Kompanie a (gp) KstN 1121a von 1 November 1943; (TE) Geschütz-Zug a (le IG) (gp) KstN 1123a gp von 1 November 1943; (TE) Pionier-Zug a (gp) KstN 1124a gp von 1 November 1943; (TE) schwerer Kanonen-Zug (7,5cm) gp KstN 1125 gp von 1 November 1943; (TE) schwerer Panzerjäger-Zug (gp) KstN 1145 gp von 1 November 1943.

PANZER-AUFKLÄRUNGS-ABTEILUNG, AUGUST 1944

Beginning in April 1944 the reconnaissance battalions were reorganised according to the frei Gliederung (fG) establishments which were gradually extended to all units of the army. The term is usually translated as free organisation but should not be taken to mean that an anything goes approach was envisaged. Rather, the new and revised KstN removed the supply and transport elements from companies and concentrated them under battalion or higher command. Although efforts were made to institute the changes, principally to 2.Panzer-Division and Panzer-Lehr-Division, it was not until 3 August 1944 that OKH directed that all Panzer divisions were to be reorganised in accordance with what was termed Gliederung Panzer-Division 44.

Stab und Stabs-Kompanie
einer Panzer-Aufklärungsabteilung (gepanzert) (frei Gliederung)
KstN 1109 (gp) (fG) von 1 April 1944

Versorgungs-Kompanie
einer Panzer-Aufklärungs-Abteilung
(gepanzert) (frei Gliederung)
KstN 1180 (gp) (fG) von 1 April 1944

Stabs-Kompanie

Sdkfz 234/1

2 x Kettenkrad

Kfz 2 VW Car

Nachrichten-Zug

The battalion's Nachrichten-Zug, or signals platoon, contained 1x Sdkfz 251/3 and 1 x VW light car with the headquarters. The five Truppen were allocated 4 x Sdkfz 251, 2 x Sdkfz 251/11 and 1 Sdkfz 250/3 halftracks.

1.Panzerspähwagen-Zug

6 x Sdkfz 234/1

2.Panzerspähwagen-Zug

6 x Sdkfz 234/1

3.Schwere Panzerspähwagen-Zug

3 x Sdkfz 234/3

1.Kompanie as
Panzerspähwagen-Kompanie c (frei Gliederung)
KstN 1162c (fG) von 1 April 1944

This establishment was similar to the others in the KstN 1162 series but with the wheeled armoured vehicles replaced by halftracks. The company was authorised a total of 9 x SdKfz 250/5, 16x SdKfz 250/9.

2.Kompanie as
Leichte Panzer-Aufklärungs-Kompanie (gepanzert) (frei Gliederung)
KstN.1113 (gp) (fG) von 1 April 1944

2 x VW light cars, 2 x Kettenkrad and 2 x Sdkfz 250/3 halftracks at the company headquarters with three platoons each equipped with 7 x Sdkfz 250/1 halftracks. The two support platoons were authorised 3 x Sdkfz 250/1, 2 x Sdkfz 250/7 and 2 x Sdkfz 250/8 vehicles.

3.Kompanie as
Panzergrenadier-Kompanie c (gepanzert) (frei Gliederung)
KstN 1114c (gp) (fG) von 1 July 1944

The company headquarters contained 2 x VW light cars, 3 x Kettenkrad and 2 x Sdkfz 251/3 halftracks. Each of the three platoons was authorised 1 x Sdkfz 251/17 and 3 x Sdkfz 251/1 halftracks. A support platoon was supposed to be equipped with 2 x Sdkfz 251/2, 2 x Sdkfz 251/9 and 1 x Sdkfz 251/17 but the inclusion of the latter was overly optimistic as the first of these vehicles did not leave the factories until November 1944.

OR

3.Kompanie as
Panzer-Aufklärungs-Kompanie (gepanzert) (frei Gliederung)
KstN.1113 (gp) (fG) von 1 July 1944

This company was organised similarly to the leichte Panzer-Aufklarungs-Kompanie but with the Sdkfz 250/8 halftracks distributed among the platoons.

4.(schwere) Kompanie

This company was made up of Teileinheiten, or parts, of other organisations and the KstN numbers can be identified by the TE prefix. In some units the Granatwerfer Zug was replaced by (Teileinheit) 12cm Granatwerfer-Zug (6 Granatenwerfer) (gepanzert) (frei Gliederung) (TE) KstN 1126 (gp) von 1.4.1944 with six towed 12cm heavy mortars.

(TE) Führer schwere Kompanie a
(gepanzert) (frei Gliederung)
KstN 1121a (gp) (fG) von 1 April 1944

1x Sdkfz 251/3 and 1 x Sdkfz 251/11 command and communications halftracks with 3 x Sdkfz 2 Kettenkrad and 2 x Kfz 1 light cars.

(TE) schwerer Kanonen-Zug (7,5cm
(gepanzert) (frei Gliederung)
KstN 1125 (gp) (fG) von 1 April 1944

1 x Sdkfz 251/3 and 1 x Sdkfz 251/1 at platoon headquarters and 6 x Sdkfz 251/9 halftracks armed with the 7.5cm L/24 gun.

(TE) 8cm Granatenwerfer-Zug a
(gepanzert) (frei Gliederung)
KstN 1126a (gp) (fG) von 1 April 1944

2 x Sdkfz 251/1, 6 X Sdkfz 251/2 halftracks equipped with 8cm mortars.

(TE) Pionier-Zug a
(gepanzert) (frei Gliederung)
KstN 1124a (gp) (fG) von 1 April 1944

1 x Sdkfz 251/2 equipped with an 8cm mortar and 7 x Sdkfz 251/7 Pionierwagen halftracks.

Although all these organisations were amended in November 1944, the most significant change was made to KstN 1125 (gp) (fG) which lost an Sdkfz 251/1 from the platoon headquarters and was allocated six Sdkfz 251/22 halftracks in place of the Sdkfz 251/9 vehicles authorised in April.

PANZER-AUFKLÄRUNGS-ABTEILUNG 2, JUNE 1944

The units of 2.Panzer-Division, including Panzer-Aufklärungs-Abteilung 2, were withdrawn from the Eastern Front in mid-December 1943 and sent to France to be rebuilt. It had been intended to reform the battalion's 1.Kompanie according to KstN 1162c of 1 November 1943 with a complete allocation of Sdkfz 234/2 armoured cars but delays in production meant that the first four vehicles were not shipped until March 1944 with the remainder allocated in the following month. Although the battalion was ordered to hand over most of the vehicles that had been brought from Russia, a significant number were retained and the organisation shown here provides a good example of how actual establishments could vary from the authorised versions. In addition, this battalion employed a unique numbering system based on Truppen rather than Züge, or platoons, with the Truppe number repeated on the hull side. Examples of this are shown in the Camouflage & Markings section and the numbers depicted here in a darker grey shade were applied in black on the actual vehicles.

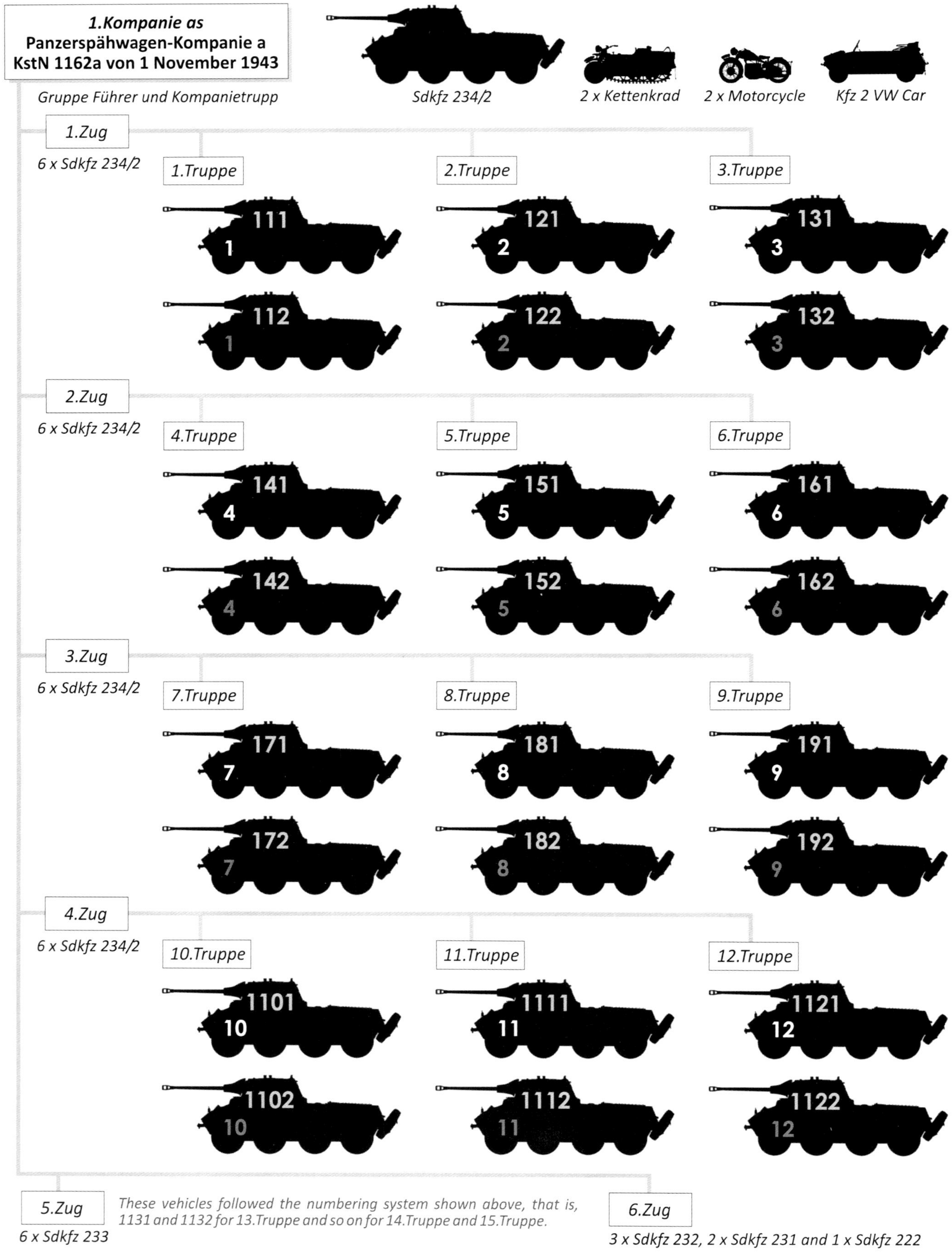

SS- PANZER-AUFKLÄRUNGS-ABTEILUNG 1, JUNE 1944

This unit, originally formed in late 1940 and attached to what was to become 1.SS-Panzer-Division, provides a good example of how armoured reconnaissance battalions were organised during the last years of the war when official establishments were modified to accommodate newly-developed equipment. It also highlights the expedients forced onto the army in times of crisis when supplies of authorised vehicles could not be guaranteed. Withdrawn from the Eastern Front in March 1944, the battalion was sent to Belgium to refit and at that time contained a Stabskompanie, four reconassiance companies, a Panzerjäger company and an infantry gun company in addition to a supply column. This establishment is shown in diagram A.

The Panzerjäger and infantry gun companies had lost all their heavy equipment in the battles in the Ukraine and were soon amalgamated into a proposed heavy company which also absorbed the Pionier-Zug from the Stabskompanie. The men of the Flak-Zug were transferred to 1.Kompanie, which was expected to be re-equipped with Sdkfz 250/9 halftracks. The sixteen Sdkfz 234/2 armoured cars, which had been shipped from the Heereszegamt in late May 1944, were all assigned to 4.Kompanie. This number is nine short of the authorised allocation, as shown in the charts on pages 60 and 63, and the shortfall was supposed to have been made up with Sdkfz 250 halftracks. The assignment of the Sdkfz 234/2 vehicles to 4.Kompanie seems to have been an initiative of the division's commander as the orders issued in October and November 1943, accompanying KstN 1162a, clearly indicate that they were to be formed into a Panzerspähwagen-Kompanie and attached to the battalion's Stabskompanie. The supply column and all the supply elements of each company were combined into a Versorgungskompanie. The reorganisation was completed by 1 June 1944 and is shown in diagram B.

A
Stab
Panzer-Aufklärungs-Abteilung
KstN 1109(gepanzert)

- *1.(Panzer-Aufklärungs) Kompanie (Volkswagen) KstN 1113*
- *2.(Panzer-Aufklärungs) Kompanie (Volkswagen) KstN 1113*
- *3. (Panzerspähwagen) Kompanie KstN 1162c*
- *4. (Panzerspähwagen) Kompanie KstN 1162*
- *5. (sch.Panzerjäger) Kompanie KstN 1140*
- *6. (Infanterie-Geschutz) Kompanie KstN 174 (modified)*
- *leichte Kolonne einer Panzer-Aufklärungsabteilung*

B
Stab und Stabskompanie
Panzer-Aufklärungs Abteilung
(gepanzert) (frei Gliederung)
KstN 1109 (gp) (fG)

- *1.(Panzerspähwagen) Kompanie KstN 1162c*
- *2.(Panzer-Aufklärungs) Kompanie KstN 1113 (gp)*
- *3. (Panzerspähwagen) Kompanie KstN 1113 (gp)*
- *4. (Panzerspähwagen) Kompanie KstN 1162a*
- *5. (schwere) Kompanie KstN 1140*
- *Versorgungskompanie KstN 1181*

C
Stab und Stabskompanie
Panzer-Aufklärungs Abteilung
(gepanzert) (frei Gliederung)
KstN 1109 (gp) (fG)

- *1.(Panzerspähwagen) Kompanie KstN 1162c*
- *2.(Panzer-Aufklärungs) Kompanie KstN 1113 (gp)*
- *3. (Panzerspähwagen) Kompanie KstN 1113 (gp)*
- *4. (schwere) Kompanie KstN 1140*
- *Versorgungskompanie KstN 1181*

One day after the June amendments were completed, orders were issued that all tank, armoured infantry, reconaissance and anti-tank units of Waffen-SS Panzer and Panzergrenadier divisions were to be reorganised according to the frei Gliederung establishments which had been introduced earlier in the year. The battalion's 4.Kompanie was disbanded and its assets, including the Sdkfz 234/2 armoured cars, were combined into a strong Panzerspähwagen-Zug which was incorporated into the Stabskompanie.

In addition, 5.Kompanie was renamed as 4.Kompanie, becoming the battalion's heavy company. But 1.Kompanie did not receive any of its allocated Sdkfz 250 halftracks and many of the company's men were drafted into two ad-hoc platoons that were meant to reinforce the Stabskompanie and be equipped with VW Schwimmwagen cars. Problems with supply hampered this decision as only about half of the required VW cars were received and one of the platoons made do with motorcycles. The lack of Sdkfz 250 halftracks also affected 3.Kompanie which was eventually outfitted with Sdkfz 251 vehicles seconded from other elements of the division. These were survivors of the winter battles on the Eastern Front and in the event only enough vehicles to equip two platoons could be scraped together. In addition, most of the company's personnel had been detached from 12.SS-Panzer-Division in May and were gradually returned to that formation to replace battle losses. The battalion's organisation prior to 15 June 1944, when the first elements left for the front, is shown in diagram C.

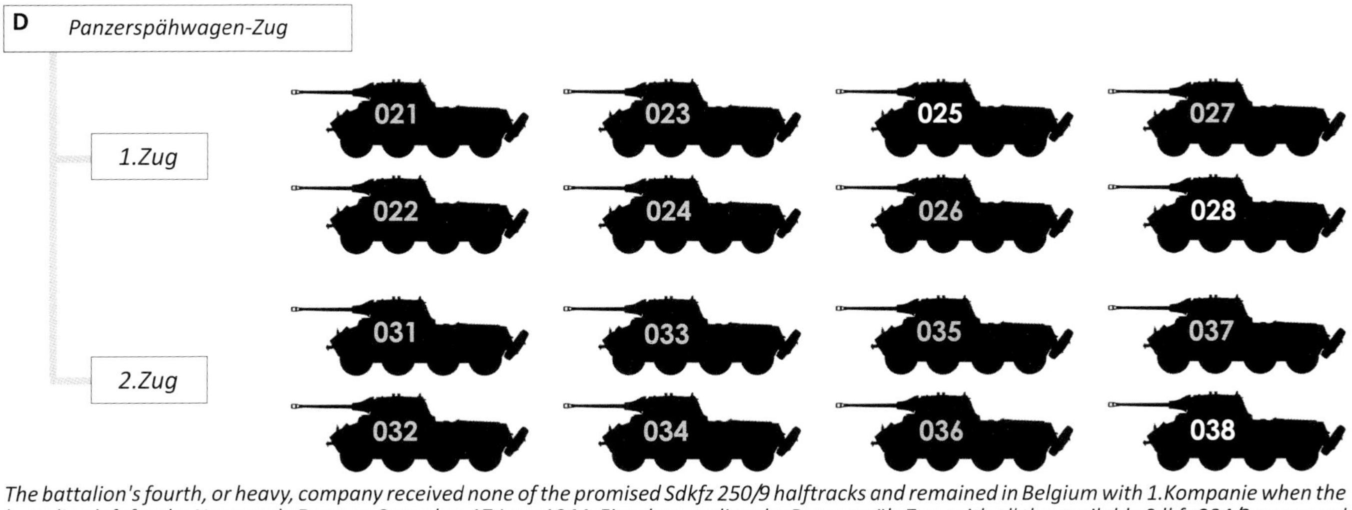

The battalion's fourth, or heavy, company received none of the promised Sdkfz 250/9 halftracks and remained in Belgium with 1.Kompanie when the battalion left for the Normandy Front on Saturday, 17 June 1944. Five days earlier, the Panzerspäh-Zug, with all the available Sdkfz 234/2 armoured cars, probably as few as ten, and the newly-formed Schwimmwagen platoon from the Stabskompanie were formed into a special Vorausabteilung, or advance group, under Hauptsturmführer Karl Böttcher and subordinated to 12.SS-Panzer-Division. This formation had been fighting around Caen since the first days of the invasion and the attachment of the Vorausabteilung has led some accounts to suggest, incorrectly, that a number of Sdkfz 234/2 vehicles were allocated to SS-PzAA 12. Shown in diagram D, above, is the Panzerspähwagen-Zug of the Stabskompanie which, despite its title, was made up of two platoons. The numbering system, while entirely possible, is speculative and based on just three confirmed examples which are depicted here in a lighter shade.

Dragon Models Ltd
B1-10/F., 603-609 Castle Peak Rd,
Kong Nam Industrial Building,
Tsuen Wan, N. T., Hong Kong
www.dragon-models.com

Tamiya Inc
Shizuoka City, Japan
www.tamiya.com

Royal Model
Via E. Montale, 19-95030,
Pedara, Italy
www.royalmodel.com

Italeri S.p.A.
via Pradazzo 6/b,
40012 Calderara di Reno, Bologna, Italy
www.italeri.com

Passion Models
This Japanese company is affiliated with MS Models Japan.
Www.passionmodels.jp

Hasegawa Corporation
3-1-2 Yagusu Yaizu,
Shizuoka 425-8711,
Japan
www.http://www.hasegawa-model.co.jp

Revell
For Revell USA -
www.revell.com
For Revell Germany -
www.revell.de/

Dan Taylor Modelworks
55 Town Hill,
West Malling,
Kent, ME19 6QL
www.dantaylormodelworks.com

Hauler
Jan Sobotka,
Moravská 38, 620 00 Brno,
Czech Republic
www.hauler.cz

Voyager
Room 501, No.411 4th Village,
SPC Jinshan District, Shanghai 200540,
P.R.China
www.voyagermodel.com

Griffon Model
Suite 501, Bldg 01, 418 Middle Longpan Rd,
Nanjing, P.R. China
www.griffonmodel.com

Aber
ul. Jalowcowa 15, 40-750 Katowice, Poland
www.aber.net.pl

E.T. Model
www.etmodeller.com

Academy Plastic Models
521-1, Yonghyeon-dong, Uijeongbu-si,
Gyeonggi-do, Korea
www.academy.co.kr

Airfix
www.airfix.com

Czech Master Kits (CMK)
Mezilesi 718/78,
19300 Praha 9,
Czech Republic
www.cmkkits.com

Panzerart
Ul. Borowa 7,
41-260 Slakow,
Poland
www.panzerart.pl

Eduard Model Accessories
Mirova 170, 435 21 Obrnice,
Czech Republic
www.eduard.com

RB Model
Powstancow Wlkp.29B,
64-360 Zbaszyn,
Poland
www.rbmodel.com

Attack Hobby Kits
Kodymova 2539/8,
158 00 Prague 5, Czech Republic
www.attack-kits.eu

OzArmour
P.O Box 51,
Burpengary, QLD, 4505,
Australia
www.ozarmour.com.au

Black Dog
Petr Polanka,
Letecká 549,
Libcice nad Vltavou, 252 66,
Czech Republic
www.blackdog.cz

Hussar productions
www.hussarproductions.com
A selection of wheel types in 1/35 scale.

Promodels / Quarter Kit
10 Passage du Charolais,
75012 Paris,
France
www.promodels.eu
This company offers a line of 1/48 scale kits and conversion sets.

In writing this book I referred extensively to the Panzer Tracts series of books created by the late Thomas L. Jentz and Hilary Louis Doyle and to SdKfz 234 *by George Parada, Mike Koenig and Stanislaw Jablonski from the Kagero Publications Top Drawings series. I would also recommend* Scouts Out: A History of German Armored Reconnaissance Units in World War II *and* Tip of the Spear: German Armored Reconnaissance in Action in World War II *both by Robert J. Edwards. I should also acknowledge the work of Martin Block, Hans Weber and the late Ron Klages whose research on unit histories and vehicle allocations would fill many volumes, and I would like to thank the modellers who graciously allowed me to publish the images of their work as well as Lisa Hooson and Stephen Chumbley, my editors at Pen & Sword. I must make special mention of Jan Zdiarsky from Eduard Model Accessories, Freddie Leung of Dragon Models and the crew at E.T. Models and to Karl Berne, Valeri Polokov and J.Howard Parker for their invaluable assistance with the photographs and period insignia.*

Photographed in Germany during a training exercise, as indicated by the white umpire's band worn on the cap of the officer in the background, this Sdkfz 234/2 armoured car is painted in a base coat of Dunkelgelb with a very fine mottling of Rotbraun and Olivgrun. The turret number is unusual and although any positive identification is not possible this may be one of the vehicles allocated to 4.Kompanie, Aufklärungs-Lehr-Abteilung based at Krampnitz.